CANT

YOU

HERE

ME

CALLING?

Cant You Here Me Calling?

Lawrence
Carter

THE SEABURY PRESS • NEW YORK

TO KATRINA

O! how thy worth with manners may I sing,
When thou art all the better part of me?

—William Shakespeare, from Sonnet 39

Nearly twenty-five years ago I remember standing on the fantail of a Navy transport as it sailed out of Puget Sound and saying to myself as the shores of the United States faded into the distance, "What the hell am I doing here?" Many times in my ministry I have felt the same sense of going out into the unknown. Certainly, accepting the rectorship of St. John's Parish in Los Angeles was one of those times. Nothing in my background had prepared me for the job. Two years in Massachusetts curacies and seven years as Episcopal Chaplain at U.C.L.A. could not be considered adequate preparation for taking over a stagnant inner-city parish church.

Mentally, however, the writings of Father Romano Guardini, the Rt. Rev. Paul Moore, Jr., and the Abbé G. Michonneau had fired my imagination and had given me a sort of missionary zeal about the life and work of Christ in the heart of the city. Another influence was Provost Ernest W. Southcott, whose writing I knew and whom I had met on one of his American visits. In the course of a drive to Santa Barbara, California, he said to me that the priest who went to work in the city shouldn't be afraid of failure. This thought supported me in those first few years at St. John's.

To write about one's work is both easy and hard. It is easy to put on paper those events and those people that have made up the largest segment of my life for the past ten years. It was John Goodbody of The Seabury Press who first suggested that I might try my hand at an account of my ministry in Los Angeles, and I am grateful to him for having given me the incentive and the opportunity.

For the most part the events described took place in St. John's. It is always in the interpretation of the events that one can err. This is even more true of one's subjective reaction to people. Most of the people referred to are real people. In some cases, to avoid hurting individuals, I have so changed names and details that wholly new characters have been created to fit the situation. Some of the people I have written about are living and a few are now dead; in other cases there is no relationship between the characters in this book and those living or dead.

The real heroes and heroines of this tale are for the most part not mentioned. They are the lay people who stuck by the parish through thick and thin. They are the ones who continued to support the church services, programs and new directions of the church. It is to them I owe my greatest debt of gratitude. Their faith, stanch ·

support and innate goodness made the stranger welcome and recognized as a person of worth and dignity. They, more than any other factor, allowed St. John's to become the comprehensive parish family it is today.

I owe an even larger debt of thanks to many friends, both clergy and laity, for their moral support and sound advice during many a dark hour of discouragement and despair. I can only mention a few names here—those unmentioned already know how grateful I am to them for their friendship and humor. Those I publicly thank here are the Right Reverends, George West Barrett, James Albert Pike, Francis Eric Bloy and finally W. Appleton Lawrence and Anson Phelps Stokes, who guided my steps into the ministry twenty years ago. Laymen to whom I am particularly indebted are Dan Mark Petrakis, Hal Harris, C. P. Grady, Miss Edith Knapp, and my deceased brother, Henry.

Finally, my thanks are due to the warm friendship and faithful support of Gwen Chandler, who has cheerfully typed and retyped this manuscript. Her efforts on my behalf have resulted in a reasonably respectable document in terms of spelling, grammar and organization.

Los Angeles   L. C.
April, 1968

CONTENTS

CANT
YOU
HERE
ME
CALLING?

PROLOGUE

Somewhere suspended between yesterday and tomorrow lies a ten-block area in the central city of Los Angeles. Until recently, the heart of its business section on Hoover Street was composed of a series of dilapidated buildings housing small shops, a launderette, an open-air market, bars and liquor stores. As this is written, they are either empty, with broken windows, or demolished by a city intent on ridding itself of an open wound to its self-respect. The only viable establishments still clinging on are the Temptation Cafe, the Gem Five and Dime, and Evy's Party Timer. The doorway of the vacant thrift shop is occupied daily, as it has been for the past ten years, by an elderly, bleary-eyed man sitting on a backless chair watching the auto and foot traffic go by.

Just south of Evy's Party Timer is a vacant lot, recently leveled. Here once stood an ungainly gray clap-board building. On the north wall of this squalid build-ing, unrelieved by windows, were written in large and uneven letters words as mysterious as those on the walls of King Nebuchadnezzar's palace. Thousands of motor-ists on their way to work coming off the freeway saw this writing and may have wondered. The words were there for the world to read, but somehow no interpreter came forward to translate them until one hot week in August, 1965, when Watts, the area only a few miles south, erupted into rioting and flames.

The words were: "CANT YOU HERE ME CALLING?"

1

||||

A DESERT IN
THE CITY'S HEART

I first saw the city fifteen years ago. By car I crossed the desert in the blazing heat of hell. Momentarily air-cooled in the squalor of a desert gambling city, on I went again into the terrible heat toward the mountains through a landscape that conformed to one's idea of total death. Not a tree, not a blade of grass—nothing except the sign that others had passed the same way, throwing empty beer cans as they went. Over the mountains and down into the coastal plains the air became cooler as the car entered the stream of traffic which stopped and started according to the traffic lights which went on for nearly seventy miles. Today a two-way freeway replaces the old route through the various towns and suburbs. But I didn't see the city begin; I entered its sprawl unaware of it until I found myself in an area I could clearly call city.

Later I came back to it by air and then I saw it in
the early dusk. The desert was almost dark as we flew
five miles up in the air. The near darkness was pricked
by a light here and there and once in a while one could
pick out an automobile making its way over the high-
way I had first driven over a few years before. A few
more lights, then the darkness of the mountains for a
moment as the plane began to let down for its landing
now only minutes away. Then lights as far as the eye
could reach. Mostly white lights with a variation now
and then of red, green and garish neon. From this
height it looked like the heavenly city. One could pick
out the highways and criss-crossing major avenues by
the moving snake of automobile lights wending its way
to and from the city.

From that distance above the ground one is de-
tached. It is only when the plane lowers so that one
can see the houses and the antlike forms of people that
one begins to feel the pull of the city. Every now and
then one can pick out specific areas around which the
traffic of the city moves—isolated sections which the
daily world passes by without a thought, yet sections
which provide homes for families, shops for pawning
their possessions for bread money. On the eastern border of one of these stands the church I serve. I tried to
make it out from the air but could only roughly mark
the area by the brick buildings of the university and the
north-south freeway which provided a spectacular dis-
play of moving lights.

From the air these areas, isolated by major traffic
patterns, look like garden spots, quiet, relatively dark,
with trees here and there lifting high above the two-
story houses. But now I knew and felt the despair I so

often felt at reaching down into the roots of it and finding nothing to justify the terrible separation between the men, women and children who live there and the obvious affluence attested to by the newly built skyscrapers and those even newer ones whose scaffolding reached high into the evening sky.

As a priest I have the ghostly power to bless and absolve; to lift high the sacred Host; to offer men and women the bread of life. But how can a mere man with even these gifts to mankind touch the lives of an alien people to make the Word known . . . to make the Word effective when the principalities and powers worked day and night to continue a culture which benefited them while the little people had no alternative but to accept the given, to accept an inadequate paycheck, an over-priced home or a relief check with which to maintain a minimum existence? How can one say, "Blessed are the poor" when one sees them accursed? What meaning have the words "Come unto me all you that travail and are heavy laden" when I know they will return to the daily grind of existence believing that nothing can change their lot—not even the divine words of assurance I have to give? How, sweet Christ? How?

The area we are considering is the so-called Hoover-Adams area, bounded on the north by Pico Boulevard, on the south by the socially correct University of Southern California, on the east by the Harbor Freeway and on the west by Vermont Avenue, in the city of Los Angeles. The street is Hoover Street between Adams Boulevard and 23rd Street. The people who live here are a scattering of elderly Caucasian men and women surviving one way or another on a combination of social security and California old-age pensions; Mexican-Americans; Negroes who find it preferable to Watts; and a few Orientals. The buildings, except for those on Adams Boulevard between Figueroa and Hoover, are owned for the most part by absentee landlords who derive rentals and pay little or no attention to city codes for building maintenance.

The police do not care much for this area. Although they bravely cruise in the prowl cars up and down Adams Boulevard, as well as up and down Hoover Street, they rarely venture into the ill-lighted sections off these main drags. After dark the police stop drivers for major and minor traffic violations, making the occupants, if Negro, stand with their arms over their heads as they search the car and persons for weapons, drugs or open liquor bottles. Illegal search and seizure? Who cares? No one will protest.

Up and down Adams Boulevard, day and night, moves an endless stream of traffic creating a roar of engine and tires, punctuated by the heavier engine noise of a bus and the siren scream of the police ambulances. Foot traffic, except for the little Hoover area, is at all times light to nonexistent. The nights are quiet off the boulevard except for the occasional shriek of a police car, the padding sound of running feet, a scream of a mugged victim and once in a while the bang of a gun fired in anger or for the hell of it.

Once this area was a proud and gilded residential section of Los Angeles, as the mansions of a bygone era attest. The owners are gone to the greener pastures of Beverly Hills and Hancock Park, or some other more elegant surrounding away from the festering sore of urban decay. In the 1920's one could guess with some accuracy that 50 per cent of the wealth of Los Angeles lived in the Hoover-Adams area. Here the *nouveau riche* with money in oil, real estate, department store enterprises, and various goods and services lived in a style to which they wanted to become accustomed. Their homes, tasteless but big, had lawns and gardens and tennis courts. They entertained lavishly as they tried to ape the modes and manners of their eastern and southern counterparts. Occasionally, visiting minor royalty from Asia and Europe were hosted to events which were pretentious if not downright vulgar.

This elite considered themselves the lords of their creation, which undoubtedly they were. They shunned the movie colony to their west except when their more elegant guests wanted to "see" Hollywood. This new nobility was sadly lacking in concern for its city and its development into one of the three largest metropolitan areas in the United States. So Los Angeles followed the classic patterns of New York, Boston, Philadelphia and Chicago as the slums developed and Angelenos watched the hordes of immigrants from the south and southwest stream into the central city. For some decades all seemed to go according to plan. The Negro population was contained in a remote area known as Watts where the famous, quaint towers of junk drew visitors. To the east was the large Mexican-American enclave. As the Negro population grew and expanded they began to move northward toward the exclusive Adams area. As the Mexican-Americans increased in numbers they pushed west until the two converging groups met and drove out the elite from their castles.

As they left their monstrous homes, the lesser middle-class homes behind the main boulevard likewise changed owners and took on new life—a life vibrant with living, laughter, yells, as Negro and Mexican-American children played in St. James Park, in the alleys and vacant lots. Men and women who lived in the divided homes scrabbled for a living by the day, by the month and, if they were lucky, by the year. Those not so lucky or skilled found their way to the welfare offices where they were screened and approved by autocratic social workers who had the power of life and death over the supplicants for relief checks. By day one can see the women off for work in the other parts of the city, in the homes that can afford cleaning women. Often one sees the man of the family reduced to the role of freemartin left to care for the children.

Everything considered, the Hoover-Adams area is a familiar problem in the decayed heart of any large city. No focal point exists, be it church or shopping center; no amusement areas except for the new and very small public playground behind the gas station at Hoover and Adams. Just people living, loving, hating, dying— barely existing—their lives barren of creativity, beauty or meaning. Meaning for most would be steady jobs, three meals a day and the death of a rapacious landlord. Where manners of a kind, servants and the American Way of Life à la Horatio Alger once flourished, there is raw life seeking existence, clawing its way day by day, frustrated and for the most part subservient to the dominant power structure of the city. But in their hearts is violence and a rage at a country, a state and a city that can give only left-handed concern to the socially and economically handicapped. After all, there

must be eight-lane freeways built to get people from
the suburbs to work, out of the city streets where human beings live—if you can call it living. We can build
topless towers for business and industry; we can ex-
pend millions on huge faceless tract homes which de-
face the countryside for thirty miles in any direction.
But we can't seem to get to the places where millions
dwell in squalor and fear with our American dream of
infinite progress.

On any given weekday, from five o'clock in the morning when the first workers leave their homes for jobs
in outlying areas or for janitorial work in the new skyscrapers downtown or up and down Wilshire Boulevard until they begin to return in the late afternoon, the
patterns of life are predictable. Women with small children go to the market at Vermont and Adams or to the
nearest (no credit) grocery store. The unemployed
men drift to one of the bars. A few of the youths play
basketball in the recreation park. The taco stand opposite Evy's Party Timer is a popular spot for some and
a loud juke box blares out rock-and-roll to compete
with the traffic sounds coming from the never-ending
stream of cars and trucks on Adams.

The evening sounds are less noisy as dinners are prepared and eaten, children put to bed and the TV turned
on for the quieter residents of the area. Others drift
about the streets, children sit on porches waiting for
parents to return late from work, and nondescript dogs
sniff at overturned trash pails. Curtains and shades are
pulled. On Hoover Street, Negro and Mexican-American groups wander about or stand on a corner talking.
Little children with notes in hand to the friendly gro-
cer go to get a quart of milk or a loaf of bread. Open

doors show people sitting at the bars talking, staring ahead of themselves or eyeing the other customers. Here and there teenage girls, trying to look much older than they are, walk down the street looking for a "two-dollar man" in their first venture in the art of prostitution. They won't last long solo as there are pimps around to look after them and their earnings. The gallants at the taco stand only look and discuss the merits of each; they don't have two dollars. An occasional university student wanders up from the ivied precincts in search of adventure and usually ends up a little drunk in one of the bars or rolled in a shabby bedroom.

This is the weekday world of Hoover-Adams. A life without a real center; a life without any but the most primary means of survival. And yet life. Life that can be renewed, reclaimed, if only someone cared. If only someone heard the cry for help. St. Paul once said, "Who will deliver me from this body of death?" Our unknown writer on the wall of a building said with equal eloquence: "Cant you here me calling?" Who are you? From what depth are you calling? Are you calling me or are you calling someone else? Who am I to hear you? Who am I to lift you out of your purgatory? There must be someone or some organization to do this. Surely you aren't my responsibility. Or are you?

2

| | | |

BRICKS WITHOUT STRAW

On the eastern border of the Hoover-Adams section of Los Angeles lies the Harbor Freeway, a never-ending stream of traffic that cuts the city in two on a north-south axis. For the little section we are dissecting it forms a barrier mightier than the Mississippi River. Beyond it to the east are small industrial establishments, wholesale businesses of a startling variety, a few shops, scruffy restaurants and bars. The homes on the other side of this moving automotive river house mostly Mexican-Americans with some Negroes and poor whites. Towering over this area is the mighty Bureau of Public Assistance, the May Company Warehouse and the Department of Motor Vehicles. Except for the stream of Mexican-American children attending St. Vincent's Roman Catholic Parochial School and their parents on their way to compulsory Sunday Mass, there is little intercourse between the two areas divided by the freeway.

Standing proudly on the eastern ramparts of the Hoover-Adams area going west we first see St. John's Episcopal Church, a monument built in the twenties to the glory of God and the vanished race which built this Renaissance basilica. Classical and austere on the exterior, it is a glory of marble and mosaic inside. Cater-corner from St. John's at Figueroa and Adams is St. Vincent's, whose tower and dome dominate the little area and whose chimes remind us of the passing hour. Built chiefly from the funds given by one of the original oil barons of Los Angeles, it is a stylized copy of provincial Spanish baroque. On the south side of the same corner is the Automobile Club of Southern California, also built in a sort of Sears-Roebuck Spanish style. Moving west down Adams we pass the former mansions of the vanished elite, now occupied by religious orders, clinics, the University of Southern California and a fraternity house. As we near Hoover Street we see a couple of new, transitory-appearing apartment houses and the marbled Christian Science Church, complete with Greek columns and a dome of mighty proportions. One mustn't forget the little section known as Chester Place, which is a conglomeration of ugly but large houses. One's eyes are startled on further inquiry into Chester Place to discover the red sandstone castle which once housed the oil milord. All Chester Place now belongs to the Roman Catholic Church and is used for a junior college run by the Sisters of St. Joseph.

If there is any "establishment" in the Hoover-Adams section it is composed of the Roman Catholic Church and its various enterprises, the Automobile Club, St. John's Episcopal Church, and the Security First National Bank just a block south of the Automobile Club.

It was in this place that I found myself on September 1, 1958, as the new rector of St. John's. I well remember the day I moved into the mansion, which was to be my rectory until it was sold three years later. It was 110° as Los Angeles was in the grip of a Santa Ana wind, which practically dries up one's throat as well as any vegetation that is left unwatered. When the movingmen were through their task it was well toward evening. Not having enough money to tip them, I offered them cold beer, which they gladly accepted and we all quenched our thirst on the imposing staircase of my new home.

After they left I sat on the front steps in shorts and a dirty T-shirt, finishing my can of beer. It was then well after dusk and I waited for a cooling wind, which didn't come. I was looking out at the traffic going back and forth, and wondered what in the world I could do to bring a ministry and new life to a parish so situated. As I turned these thoughts over in my head and rested my body, which was hot and tired, a police car stopped by the entrance of the rectory. An alert young policeman came bounding up the path to the steps where I was sitting. He wished to know who I was, why the front door was open, and a lot of other questions which clearly told me that he thought I was some sort of a tramp who had probably broken into the house. I identified myself and after some conversation convinced him that I was the rightful occupant of the house, and he departed somewhat reluctantly. That was my first night as rector of St. John's Episcopal Church.

A church is people, not a building. This was and still

is my belief. Often the building itself can be a barrier to community, and worse, can become the idol which replaces the reality. Then the building becomes the focus of worship and the people become inward-directed. For each, especially the old-timers, the building represents something they have given . . . something they have worked for in its creation, and somehow their self-image is there in the stone, mortar and wood of the very fabric of the building. The result of this syndrome is that the individual, having placed all that is precious to himself in the building, sees any threat to the *status quo* as a personal threat.

I cannot forget my experience with the devil's first temptation at St. John's. It happened late one afternoon in the first month I was there when there was no one around. I went in the church by the front door and was once again overwhelmed by the architecture and the beauty of stained glass and mosaic, and I said to myself, "This is mine." I walked up the main aisle slowly, savoring the sheer magnificence of the place, up to the high altar which glowed with shine of marble and gilt of wood-carving high above it. A glory for me to use, to be a setting for my ministry. Here I would celebrate the Holy Eucharist, here I would preach the Word, and here the glorious organ and choir would lend their skill to whatever I did or said.

And then I turned around and saw the row upon row of empty pews. I was overwhelmed again and wondered if we would ever fill these pews and if indeed I had anything to give sufficient to accomplish this miracle. I remembered my second Sunday when something like a total of ninety people sat where some eight hundred could be comfortably seated, and felt the cold hand of defeat and failure. I couldn't do it. No one could. The tide toward the suburbs and the total separation between St. John's and the community seemed insuperable obstacles to any accomplishment, large or small, in this parish.

Here's the church and here's the steeple, look inside and see all the people. This childish rhyme and finger game came into my head as I sat in an empty pew and began to think of the people I had met so far. First, there was the Vestry, that ruling committee of every Episcopal Church, who for the most part are the parochial power of our communion. Sometimes comic, sometimes tragicomic heroes, and sometimes a faceless group which finds it easier to do what the rector thinks rather than to exert their own dedication and influence to guide the priest.

My first real meeting with the power structure of the parish had been within a few days of my arrival. It was at a very elegant dinner party given for me and everyone was very nice to me as well as to each other. It was composed of vestrymen and their wives and the chosen faithful, notable for either their contributions or their service. All the guests were good members of the parish, numbering some twenty-five or thirty. We chatted over cocktails and the buffet dinner. They were too well mannered to grill me on various points of view. I wasn't even asked what political party I belonged to. It was a nice evening and one I will long remember for its warmth, its genuine concern for me as a person and its unspoken hope that in me they had found the man to lead them into a new era. Unfortunately for them, the world moves forward, not backward. Their idea of a new era was one in which the pews would be filled as in the old days of the rector-builder when St. John's stood for the good things of life and an insurance policy for eternity. This isn't to say that they were not religious people or people of faith. Obviously they thought of themselves as such and undoubtedly they were. But even in that pleasant and agreeable social gathering I realized that what lay ahead of them in terms of the future of the parish would be vastly different from what they expected from me. I knew I could not be a faithful shepherd as they understood it. For the grass of their pasture was exhausted and faithfulness would have to mean leading them into new and unknown fields which would expose them to a new reality, both religious and social. As I drove home to the rectory I thought that this could be possible by not being radical in my first moves and by accepting their very real offer of friendship and support. We can grow together, I thought rather fatuously, and nothing is impossible!

St. John's had been, unhappily, a harshly divided group of people in the upheaval which preceded my arrival. The immediate job, as I saw it, was to try to heal the wounds in this congregation and to be first of all a pastor who would help to reconcile differences so we could become united in our service to the one Lord we all served. I refused to listen to tales of the former rector or the behavior of this vestryman or that. The extent of the wounds on this congregation were best found in the testimony of the parish roll, which showed that no fewer than one hundred persons had left the parish permanently prior to my arrival. This presented a severe problem in terms of sheer numbers, to say nothing of the money they took with them to other parishes in the city and suburbs. My wonderful German secretary came to me one morning and announced that after a careful perusal and study of the parish roll she could find fewer than five hundred persons who could be considered bona fide members. This was a blow, as the statistics for the previous year represented nearly fifteen hundred. I kept this fact to myself, feeling that any general announcement would detract from the psychological boost the parish had received in getting a new priest.

Outside of the beauty of the church building itself, the other facilities left a great deal to be desired. No central office and reception room for the necessary work existed. A gnomelike little man, introduced to me as the financial secretary, sat in a musty, dark office off the lovely patio. He doled out money and stamps and paid the bills sixty to ninety days after they were due. Next to his office was the men's choir dressing room. On the opposite side of the patio was an office for the secretary and one for me. The public lavatories flanked one of the walls of the patio. The rector's office was next to the ladies' room, which made for some embarrassment as the toilets thundered like a Niagara whenever used.

While the architecture of the patio was attractive in design and detail, the patio was barren of plant or flower. In fact there was a forbidding atmosphere which chilled the person seeking ghostly counsel. Realizing that I must act while the good feeling existed between me and the powers of the parish, I insisted that the so-called financial office and men's choir room be thrown together to provide a suitable reception area. There was some grumbling, but the money was found and an attractive office with sofas and chairs for parishioners and others was created.

More improbable than the facilities provided the rector of St. John's was the human furniture of the place. This was found in the persons of a semiretired Chinese priest and family, and the Irish-American sexton and his wife. They lived on the premises in apartments provided in the rambling, worn-out structure of the parish house. On prowling around, I found a third apartment, which had formerly been used by a curate. Now the budget couldn't provide the rector with a full-time assistant and Father Chung was able to assist with the daily Masses and do limited calling on the elderly.

The first hint that all wasn't well in this household of God came one day when the Sheas came to me with fire in their Irish eyes and announced that they couldn't stand it any longer and wanted to leave. I wondered what in the world I had done to produce this state of affairs as I had gone out of my way to be pleasant to them. Upon further inquiry I got the rather mysterious answer, "It's them feathers."

"Feathers," I asked?

"Yes, pigeon feathers. George has to sweep them up every day," they replied.

I explained to them that pigeons were a problem in any city and there wasn't much I could do about feathers which drifted into the rear courtyard between the church building and the parish house. To my astonishment Mrs. Shea said with venom, "Them feathers come from Father Chung's pigeons that he keeps on the roof." This seemed so highly improbable that I asked why they thought that the Chungs raised pigeons. As if telling a child some well-known fact of life, Mrs.

Shea said, "Father Chung, as he calls himself, and his wife raise the pigeons and kill 'em. Then they eat them in their heathen way." This left me with the hilarious mental picture of Father and Mrs. Chung covered with feathers and blood, eating their victims raw, and I became convulsed with laughter. To my surprise, the Sheas joined me, and went off mollified when I promised to look into the matter and see what I could do.

Obviously, a call on the Chungs was in order and this fascinating side of their life made it necessary. So that afternoon I ascended the staircase which led to the clergy apartments and rang the bell at the Chungs' door. There was no answer so I decided to step out onto what appeared to be a small outdoor area used for hanging laundry, as two large sheets were hanging on a line. Out of curiosity I pushed the sheets apart and gazed on a sight the like of which I have never seen before or since. There, laid out on a camp cot, was an ancient Chinese crone enjoying the sun, stark naked. I hastily let the sheets fall together and took my leave as quickly as I could. Back in my office I relapsed into hysterical laughter, in which state my secretary found me a few minutes later. When I could pull myself together I told her and she too went completely to pieces in what can only be described as giggles.

These were conditions for which none of the books on "how to" do work in an inner-city parish had prepared me. Another was the financial role I was expected to play. Aside from a debt I didn't realize the church had incurred over the past few years, another aspect of our handling of financial affairs which concerned me was the method of paying regular bills. On the theory that it was cheaper to use other people's money, suppliers, except of phone service and utilities, were paid on a ninety-day basis. The theory was fine but I soon found our credit was nil. There were rather unpleasant phone calls from irate creditors demanding payment. I had four calls the day after the newspaper carried a story on my installation as the new rector.

3

||||

"O LORD, FOR
A SECOND DANIEL"

The first few months turned into a year with little or no
time for a long view of the role of the church. Little by
little we achieved a semblance of order in terms of
daily work and administration. The financial situation continued to be acute. The biggest problem was a
row of rundown storefronts on Figueroa Street which
the church owned. Half the stores were vacant and the
few which held on had tenants consisting of a couple
of restaurants, a barber shop, a dress shop, and a rather
dubious wholesale furniture shop. The whole thing
was an eyesore as the church hadn't invested a nickel
to maintain the property except when the roofs began
to leak. As this business property ran around the Adams
corner almost to the church building itself, it was a
pretty poor advertisement for the parish. It didn't take

me long to realize the fact that the tenants hated St. John's in general and its Vestry in particular for the high rents and lack of maintenance. I was not received by them very cordially.

At a meeting of the Vestry toward the end of the first year I suggested that this was one time when bad theology, as well as bad business practices, resulted in a pretty poor thing for the parish. After months of discussion and negotiations, a lease was signed with an oil company which included demolishing all the existing buildings at their expense for the erection of a gas station. This agreement also provided for extra Sunday parking, although we certainly didn't need it at that point. A few people clucked at the idea of having a gas station on church property, but when told of the revenue from rent and gas sales they were soon quieted.

In the State of California the rector of a parish is not only a church official but also president of a state-approved nonprofit corporation. This seemed to me to say that I had additional responsibilities to my pastoral and spiritual duties as a priest. This led me to a lengthy study of the church finances, its properties, as well as such items as income and outgo, to say nothing of the bank loan of some seventy thousand dollars. It soon became quite apparent that the interest being paid on debts and mortgages constituted a major drain on income. Obviously, income had to be increased and expenses reduced if we were ever to move toward the goal of a going fiscal concern.

All this may not seem to have much to do with the God business, but without a somewhat-better-organized financial base it was impossible to proceed with the job of determining the proper role of the parish. I made many, many mistakes in terms of both judgment and leadership. I first instituted a system of requisitions for all expenditures of money which had to have my approval. This was particularly galling to the sexton, who was used to ordering as he pleased. But it did succeed in cutting down unnecessary spending. We had a financial campaign, run by a professional, which was nothing but sheer disaster, as it cost more money than we got in return. A few years later we found that running our own fund drive produced more results at less cost. As can be seen, finances were a nightmare. Almost every meeting of the Vestry was devoted to discussions of money and expenses.

Finally some sort of order came into existence. The rector assumed full responsibility for all approved budget items, and Vestry approval was required for extra-budget items. Then after three years the huge mansion on Adams Boulevard, which had been left to the parish and which I used as a rectory, was sold to the Roman Catholic Archbishop. With the proceeds we paid off all the debts, mortgages and bank loans, and invested the remainder in a trust fund in memory of the donor of the property. But all this took time . . . years in fact. Nothing moved very fast at St. John's. It took four years to get a small piece of land west of the church and adjacent to the oil station turned into lawn. It took six years to get modern office equipment, such as typewriters, addressing equipment and duplicating machines. Actually, the addressing equipment took a bit longer—seven years. The old machine resembled one of the instruments of torture found in the Medieval Museum in Nürnberg. When Father Chung was finally gathered to his ancestors, I had to address the enve-

lopes for some parish mailing and found that without
great manual dexterity, which I lacked, one could
smash one's hand or fingers with the greatest of ease.
When the company was called upon to do some minor
repairs they marveled that this piece of antique junk
was still in operation after nearly fifty years.

It was amazing to me how a group of prominent
businessmen, who would not tolerate inefficient and
outdated office equipment in their own offices, could
delay, haggle and obfuscate when it came to bringing
the church up to date. They often reminded me of a
large chemical company I worked for in New York
many years ago. That company threw out all the rules
of good business when it came to one of its subsidiary
companies, which it treated as a man treats a willful
mistress. So was the church regarded. Only in this case
it was a mistress to whom they no longer gave their full
attention or concern.

Behind all my struggles with the material aspects
of the parish lay the conviction that without sound
management, modern communication equipment, and
first-rate personnel, St. John's would continue to stag-
nate and decay. Above all else, we needed more clergy
to help with the pastoral side of the ministry. Luck was
on my side when a young Irishman, a priest of the
church, was appointed chaplain to the Episcopal stu-
dents at the University of Southern California. He
joined my efforts in the conduct of the services, preaching and doing considerable pastoral counseling. His
sharp wit and incisive preaching were a great boost
to the effort. In addition, I needed a full-time curate.
While relatively few in numbers, the people of the

parish were spread throughout the width and breadth
of the city of Los Angeles—some two hundred square
miles. It sometimes took me four hours to make three
hospital calls, to say nothing of home visits and what
passes for normal pastoral calling.

One of the aspects of inner-city parochial work which
baffled me was the lack of warmth, personally, on the
part of the majority of the members. At first, quite obviously, they were taking me on speculation. That is
to say, they weren't buying, nor were they willing to be
sold, after their recent experience with rectors. To overcome this I had a number of social gatherings before
we sold the huge old rectory. Once the whole parish was
invited for supper. Nearly two hundred came. Another
time everyone was invited for a New Year's reception. I
instituted regular Sunday night suppers at the rectory
as well as the instruction classes and various social
events put on by the women of the parish. None of this
seemed to bring me any closer to the people. They came
to eat and drink and they went away with never any
reciprocal action on their part. It was lonely—damned
lonely. Once in a while there would be a breakthrough
when I attended a family at a death or serious illness.

I remember one experience which could have made
one rather cynical. The mother of a vestryman was in
dire personal trouble. The husband had deserted her.
The four children were all of school or college age. And
the money was gone. We arranged a Vestry meeting to
loan this woman in distress the money necessary to tide
her over until she could get a job teaching in the public
school system. To make a long story short, she soon got
the necessary job and was back on her feet. From that

day to this she never made any effort to repay the loan of several hundred dollars, though she greets me very nicely whenever I happen to run into her. Not long after this, about the time that the Negro membership in St. John's began to increase, her son transferred to another parish.

When the Vestry first interviewed me with the idea of securing me for their rector, the matter of integration came up almost immediately. They had some Negro members but clearly didn't want a large increase in Negro membership. I stated that I couldn't be rector of a parish that wasn't open to all people who wanted to become members. I stated that I had no intention of a big membership drive for Negroes, but it was obvious from the makeup of the adjacent neighborhoods that in the natural course of events we would have increasing Negro growth in the parish. As this became a fact in the course of time, tensions began to develop. A few left the parish, giving various reasons for their departure, but curiously enough, some continued and still continue to give money at Christmas to the parish of their younger days. Today Negroes constitute a third or more of the parish. Like their fellow Caucasian members, they come from all stations of life and represent many different professions. Today they serve in all aspects of our parish life, including the Altar Guild and the all-powerful Vestry. To give the old-timers credit, the ones who stayed have accepted the new order with varying states of grace, but the fact is that those who have not either removed themselves or been removed by death have accommodated themselves to the fact that Negroes are a part of our life. I well recall one moment of rebellion at a Vestry meeting. One member said it was all very well to have Negro members but they contributed only nickels and dimes in the collection plate. Fortunately I was prepared for this one. I said quietly that an examination of the pledges received from a sampling of the regular Negro members of the parish showed that they contributed on the average more dollars per week than anyone on the Vestry save our generous tycoon. It was never referred to again either in private or in a Vestry meeting.

A person who gave the establishment more trouble than any Negro was a young man of Jewish origin who became a confirmed member of the Church after many years of soul-searching and many conferences with me long before I became rector of St. John's. Originally he had been baptized in a Roman Catholic Church because he played on their school basketball team. His zeal as a convert, his clever mind and sharp insight into the human structures involved in parish management and life threatened almost every vestryman, as well as the old-time parish leaders. He involved himself deeply with me in my efforts to bring a small group of new Negro members and new white members of the parish into a discussion situation at the rectory on weekday evenings. We called ourselves an apostolate and studied not only various aspects of the Christian faith, but also quite honestly and frankly discussed the problems of being black and white and the subtle and not so subtle anxieties of integration. His popularity got him elected to the Vestry ultimately, which coincided with the election of the first Negro to the sacred Vestry of St. John's. When this happened there were cries of

"dirty pool" and accusations of politiking. He took it
all in his stride with a real degree of humor and a curious attitude of humility. He fulfilled his role with
faithfulness and diligence and many times called me
to account for things he questioned in my conduct of
parish life and work.

He carried a heavy personal cross which very few
persons knew until he died. Divorced a few years before, he conducted a business which consisted of
the management and reorganization of small businesses. What more perfect man for the job of working with a crumbling parish! Few people realized that
his days were limited, that he was fighting a silent
and brave battle against a form of cancer which would
ultimately kill him. Cobalt treatments and radical chem-
otherapy failed to inhibit his efforts on behalf of his
business and his church. The last year of his life he
served as senior warden of St. John's. This was not without its own particular drama and amusing aspects.

The peculiar law in our particular diocese of the Episcopal Church is that the rector has the obligation to appoint the senior warden each year rather than make
it a matter of popular election at the Annual Meeting.
The December before I appointed Hal senior warden
I was entertained at lunch at the California Club, the
ne plus ultra of Los Angeles. Those present represented
the fading power structure of the Vestry. The luncheon
was overtly given to discuss the financial picture of St.
John's and to work out the general fiscal direction for
the coming year. All of a sudden I found myself under
attack. My sins of omission and commission, both real
and imaginary, were brought out. Then the cat was let
out of the bag. One of the men, a major contributor in

terms of money, said he hoped I wasn't going to make a mistake in my selection of a senior warden for the coming year. In fact he stated that if I should select that "Jew boy," he would lose faith in my rectorship and consider withdrawing from the parish. Suspecting that his threat might be bluff, I said as politely as I could at the moment that I had to select the man I thought best for the job and would announce his name at the Annual Meeting in January at the regular time. But there it was. Cold and bare. I could yield to the threat and be sure of the support so needed to keep things going or I could stick to my guns. As I had already asked Hal if he would accept the appointment and he had assented, I felt as if I had already crossed the Rubicon. But I was worried. Without the funds given by this one man, I would have to fire the curate and drastically cut the parish program. I thanked the host for the martini and the lunch and we all left with a semblance of friendliness. I am sure they thought the pressure would work and I am equally sure they thought that what they were doing was for the good of the parish as they understood it. But to me it was an ugly moment of truth.

Soon after, I had an informal meeting with a number of the new leaders of the parish, both white and black, and told them of this luncheon and its implications. To my great joy they supported my choice wholeheartedly and vowed to give me all the aid I needed in what appeared to be the dark days ahead.

It is a custom which I introduced to have the Annual Meeting in the church itself. On the great day we went through the routine business of reports, with the retiring senior warden sitting on my right. Then came the moment when I announced the new senior warden and

I could see all eyes on me—friendly eyes, hostile eyes, questioning eyes, unquestioning eyes and, finally, the eyes of my wife. She knew of the struggles involved. I went through the usual speech, thanking the retiring warden for his labors. In fact I laid it on a bit thick. Perhaps too thick. But I was sincere, as he had been senior warden when I was called as rector to St. John's and we had been through many trying times together. I thought I knew the measure of the man, but as it turned out I didn't. When I announced my selection of Hal as senior warden, he gathered up his papers, stiffly shook hands with Hal as he came forward to take the chair beside me, and strode out of the church. It turned out that his departure was for good.

This was an important day for St. John's. It was the day that the self-perpetuating power of the old guard was broken forever. It was the day that the new people for the first time in the seven years of my pastorate had a majority voice in the management of the church. It was the real turning point when eyes became focused on the present and the future rather than on the good old days which never were as good as they appeared in retrospect.

Hal died in Cedars of Lebanon Hospital on New Year's Day the following year, the day he officially went out of office as senior warden. During the last months of his life he continued to direct the affairs of his office, as well as help me with major decisions in church matters, until mercifully he fell into a coma which ended the wracking pains of the disease, and his soul returned to God. His funeral was a full Requiem Eucharist with choir and a large attendance. Vestrymen, old and new, carried his coffin into the church and out again at the conclusion of the Mass. In a strange way his death brought together again those who had been divided by his entrance into parish affairs. That is what he would have wanted, for he was a kind man and one who knew that love, rather than bylaws and dollars, was the coin of God.

4

"CONFESSION AND COUNSELING BY APPOINTMENT"

That's what the bulletin board in front of the church said when I first came to St. John's and that's what it says today. In the beginning I was fooled by the outward trappings of catholicity of my new parish. I mentally prepared myself to spend every Saturday afternoon hearing the confessions of the faithful. As it turned out, confessions were made before Christmas and Easter and occasionally in between—never in summer! Many an Easter and Christmas Eve I sat waiting for the penitents and few came. I even preached on it in the belief that confession is good for the soul. It wasn't long before I learned that the stated times for hearing confessions was a fine time for reading and even sermon preparation. In his recent book, Father James Kavanaugh has some scathing things to say about the Roman

Catholic confessional system and at the same time lauds the Anglican concept that "some do, all may and none must." However, I would say that the Anglican idea and use of the confessional could do with some updating and reinterpretation. I got awfully tired of hearing about the minutiae of sin such as mind wandering during Mass, masturbation, the minor use of profanity and failure to say morning and evening prayers. The sins of racial prejudice, arrogance, and the use of persons as things, never seemed important to the penitents.

After a while I found that my usefulness as a pastor was negated by hearing confessions in terms of personal problems. What is said in confession can never be referred to by the priest unless the penitent brings it up again in a counseling situation. So I relegated most of the confessional work to the curate, who rather fancied himself as the only remaining Catholic in the world—particularly after Vatican Council II. He continued to worry about eating before receiving Holy Communion, the souls of unbaptized infants, and all the other things a good Catholic should worry about, even including contraception which in the Anglican Communion is not a sin.

On the other hand, the counseling work, whether by appointment or not, was real, gutsy and lively by comparison with the dull rote of confessional sins. Here men and women came with their problems. First of all came the steady stream of beggars, professional and otherwise, who are the bane of the downtown parish. In the mysterious way in which word gets around in that circle of our society, the news went out that a new priest had come to St. John's—and they came in droves. At first I heard the stories and gave a dollar here and there until I realized a striking similarity in all their tales of woe. They all seemed to have a job waiting for them in San Pedro or Long Beach and needed the money for bus fare. Another amazing fact was that when couples came with their children in a broken-down car from Arkansas, Texas or Illinois, they had always enough money to make the long trip to California but all arrived broke. The other gimmick was to come Saturday morning when the welfare bureau was closed for the weekend, with a story about not being able to get their checks until Monday. Granted the inefficiency of some welfare workers and the system in general, the law of averages would combat the theory that so many checks went astray or got held up exactly at four o'clock Friday afternoon.

A number of cases stand out in my mind. The first was a runaway couple who had got married in spite of parental objections. They came from Michigan. A more attractive and appealing couple would be hard to imagine. They sought me out because they were members of the Episcopal Church where they came from and they had no place else to turn. They were living in a scruffy motel down the street. For a first effort I bought them groceries instead of giving them money, as I had been stung so many times in the past. They were so grateful that it was heartwarming. Then I loaned them money for gasoline and carfare so they could go to various job interviews. Soon they were located in jobs. They came to church regularly for a while and then disappeared. Perhaps the letter I wrote their rector in the midwest brought about a family reconciliation. I never knew. But a couple of years ago

I got a money order in the mail addressed to me with no other indentification than the postmark "Detroit." I rather like to think that this unidentified check came from the couple as repayment for what the church had done for them.

It is a funny thing about money given to people in need by the church. I suppose that over the years of my pastorate in the inner city I have dispensed something close to five thousand dollars. In only two cases in my memory has money been repaid to me or to the parish. One was the case just mentioned and the other was equally rewarding in terms of the insights it gave me into the bravery of the human spirit struggling under great handicaps.

One day I was sitting in my office, which is always open for all the world to walk into, when a fine-looking young Negro, accompanied by his wife, knocked on the door. Did I mind if he talked with me a few minutes? I said, "Come in." At first I thought it was the same old story about having arrived in Los Angeles with no job and no money. Then I began to sense something different about this young man. As I questioned him I realized that here indeed was a refreshing change from the usual grifter, black or white, who came with outstretched hand. His grandfather had been raised on a tenant farm in the Deep South, his father had been raised on the same farm under the same conditions and this man, the third generation, had likewise had this heritage of poverty and marginal life presented to him as the accepted way of life for him. He was married and had three children. Very hesitantly he told me that he wanted a different life for himself and particularly for his children. He had come to California to find this opportunity and to find a place where his children could go to good schools and college. He had only a few years of formal education behind him.

In all honesty I had to tell him that segregation in Los Angeles was as real as it was in the Deep South; it only appeared different. I also had to tell him bluntly that without education and a skill he would probably be worse off in our highly technological society than he was on the farm. He stubbornly refused to consider returning to the South. So I suggested that he look for a daytime job, any job, and start going to the adult education classes conducted by the city schools. I helped this couple with money for nearly a month and they too disappeared from sight. I am afraid that when I thought of them, I thought I had really been taken and chalked the whole thing up to experience. Just four years later a well-dressed Negro couple came to my office one afternoon. I had a hard time recognizing the blue-jeaned young man and the calico-dressed young woman of four years before. When they recalled themselves to me I had difficulty keeping my surprise from showing, particularly when they gave me a hundred and twenty-five dollars in repayment for the money I had loaned them when they first arrived in Los Angeles.

The story is remarkable because, unhappily, it is so rare. The man had indeed got jobs to keep the family alive—washing cars, washing dishes, casual labor, and the whole gamut of part-time work so familiar to the unskilled worker in our society. But he had hung on and at night he had gone to school to learn the basic skills of reading, writing and mathematics. He had then gone to school to learn automotive mechanics. All during this period his wife had taken in laundry to help keep things going. Somehow he developed a specialty in working on foreign cars. He had a steady, well-paying job. The wife no longer took in laundry and they had moved out of a ghetto into a somewhat more pleasant area and were buying their own home. Their thanks to me and the church was so real and heartfelt that I had a hard time keeping the tears out of my eyes.

So many faces pass through my mind as I write this. Broken lives, broken spirits, and broken bodies— broken by a society which prefers to push the dirt under the rug rather than learn how to heal and restore the human spirit. It costs less to give money to maintain people on minimum subsistence than to spend more and rehabilitate. And we are a practical people, we Americans. There into my office came tragedy, degradation, and occasionally humor to relieve the gloom and despair which engulfs any pastor in his work. One such episode concerned the man who came in one day, saying that he couldn't keep his false teeth in when he had a "spell." In fact, he said he felt one coming on. Fascinated, I watched a most remarkable performance. He began to shudder all over. Suddenly his face became contorted and his upper and lower dentures shot out into his waiting hand. It was such a skillful and unique method of extorting money from people, I gave him a dollar.

The problem of alcohol is one which every minister wrestles with endlessly. Well- and low-born men, women and young adults, the pattern always seems to be the same unless the alcoholism is psychogenic in origin. Alcoholics Anonymous offers the only solution to so many, and yet how few take advantage of that re-creative fellowship! One of my few "successes" started a chapter of A.A., which meets now regularly in the parish house. However, it is a sad commentary that today there are no members of St. John's parish involved in this program, even though its meetings are well attended.

In fact it must be said that the bulk of the pastoral work of a downtown church is totally unconnected with the regular members of any one particular church. Most people who come for help are either from other parishes or from none. Those from other parishes come because of the comparative anonymity of the downtown church. Those from no church are there because there is no place else to turn.

Drug addicts present a difficult problem because of the very nature of drug addiction. Synanon offers the only program which is designed really to help the addict. I take my hat off to that tough-minded and dedicated group. It takes an act of the will on the part of the addict to turn his life over to the Synanon program. It is utter folly to give either an alcoholic or a narco money, but the pastor can on occasion develop a relationship of trust which can lead the person to the possibility of a cure. The same can also be said of those mentally sick or psychologically disturbed. Priests and ministers who take upon themselves the awesome task of trying to lead a sick person out of a neurotic or psychotic state are fools or charlatans. Only a qualified clinical psychologist or psychiatrist should attempt to cope with an emotionally sick person. I say this because every now and then a minister or priest suddenly decides that he is God's gift to such persons and attempts to deal in depth with the explosive and dangerous forces which play such a large part in mental sickness. Sometimes they have attended the Jung Institute in Zurich, Switzerland, for a few months or a year and return to heal the world and his brother. They use the jargon of the profession and generally do vastly more harm than good. Very often they are disturbed persons themselves and are acting out their own needs in a fashion which benefits neither man nor God.

The only role a minister can and should play with the mentally sick is to try to win the confidence of the person to such an extent that a referral to a competent psychiatrist can be made. To be able to detect the symptoms of mental illness is necessary for the contemporary pastor, but to try to go further than that is to court disaster for the person and, sometimes, for the pastor. I well recall a minister who was shot and killed by a man he was counseling in "depth." Another sad case was a young man who ended up in bed with his lady "client," which resulted in his dismissal from the ministry. To a man going into the ministry I can say with absolute authority of experience: Leave depth psychology to the professionals and find a few cooperative and able professionals to whom referrals can be made.

Homosexuals and prostitutes constitute problems in our society. The former usually do not want to be helped and seem to revel in the fact that they are different. They are generally paranoid in terms of their position vis-à-vis the straight world. They are also often sorry for themselves. And usually they come to the minister when their "lover" has deserted them or when there is real danger of exposure that would jeopardize their jobs. Police activity in this subculture only seems to aggravate the unpleasant symptoms of the abnormality. They all need help, but few seek it except as a palliative in times of stress. In my experience only a few are willing to undergo the agony of depth analysis. The few in my experience who have had the courage to do this have emerged healed, redeemed and useful members of society. Sometimes they have married happily, and sometimes not.

Prostitutes, on the other hand, offer a somewhat more honest and wholesome situation. For many it is a completely satisfactory way of life. Few operate without a protector in the form of a pimp, though a few seem to be able to get along on their own. One of the more tragic cases I recall is that of a nice-appearing, corn-fed young woman of about twenty-eight. She had come to Los Angeles to be on her own and had pretty well broken with her family, who lived near St. Paul, Minnesota. Her unconventional attitude toward her sex life had made life an embarrassment to her elderly parents from her late teens until her departure for the West Coast. Reacting against a strong Scandinavian background, she took a room in a boardinghouse in the largely Negro south-central area of our city. There she had met and fallen in love with a young Negro. As she told me the story, she soon moved out of the boardinghouse into an apartment with her lover. The problems of a white girl living with a Negro in a Negro section were ignored in the first rosy glow of the relationship. He even talked of marriage, but that never progressed beyond the talk. Several months after their affair began, he told her that he was broke and needed money desperately to pay off a gambling debt.

He told her that his life was in danger if he didn't pay. She said she would start looking for a regular job, but he said he had a better idea. That is how she started "doing tricks" for her man. That he was nothing better than a common pimp who could use her never crossed her mind then, and when it did her dependence on him was too great for her to break away.

She came to see me at the urgent request of her sister, who was worried about her proposed "marriage" to a Negro. Apparently she had written her sister to stick the knife a little further into her conventional and bewildered family. Several months later the sister appeared at my office. It turned out that she was a fine young woman who had moved from the ranks of amateur tennis players to the professional circuit. Her life was set and her retirement from the exhibition courts was imminent due to her impending marriage to an insurance broker. She had come to Los Angeles to rescue her sister from what she correctly had guessed to be a life of sin. She was hurt and baffled by the fact that her sister rejected her offer of help and appeared quite satisfied with her kind of life. We talked several times, including a final session with both sisters present. There was no meeting of minds. Appeals in behalf of the elderly parents fell on deaf ears. We both tried our best to point out where she was headed but to no avail. Finally, the prostitute left, saying that it was getting late and she had to go to work. The sister cried quietly for a few moments and left, thanking me for all I had done, which so far as I could see was exactly nothing. I never saw either woman again, though every now and then I receive a check made out to St. John's from an address in Minnesota.

In a sense, this is a typical pastoral situation of an inner-city parish. You come into the middle of a situation to which there is no apparent solution. The principals disappear after a few interviews, and the pastor never knows the end of the story. Sometimes we help, sometimes we don't, and sometimes we never know.

5

| | | | |

THE STRUCTURE AND
THE REALITY

The days stretched into weeks and the weeks into months and the months inevitably into years. Attempts to provide a stable ministry, a parish church which sometimes appeared like one, increased membership, including a fair number of Negroes; all seemed to augur well for the future of this venerable (for California) institution. Even the congregation looked better. All the aspects of a normal parish appeared present. The women met in various groups, the Altar Guild functioned, instruction classes were taught in the faith and even a Sunday school was conducted every Sunday for some fifty to seventy-five children. To be sure, there continued to be an annual deficit which was met by dipping into legacies that hadn't been tucked into trust funds. We shone like stars in the eyes of the

diocesan treasurer, for we paid our full due to the diocese and the national Church after begging for a
reduction commensurate with our reduced circumstances.

The inclusion of Negroes in increasing numbers into
the people of St. John's took place with little or no overt
opposition by the white membership. Occasionally one
could hear a bitter comment about "them." Several
complained to me that "they" ought to go to their own
church. The Vestry occasionally voiced fears that
"they" would overrun the parish and drive out the Caucasians. As this didn't happen, and as Caucasians continued to join the church too, there was a state of armed
neutrality and forbearance.

That nearly one third of the parish consisted of
Negroes and that they were beginning slowly and hesitantly to take their places in various organizations
didn't mean that, except on the most superficial level,
integration had taken place. It must have taken heroic
courage on the part of the first Negro women to do their
share in the para-sacramental liturgy of the after-
church coffee hour dispensing cookies and coffee to the
congregation. But they did and they stuck at it, sometimes surpassing the white women in their effort to produce interesting and tasty snacks. This was regarded
by the regulars who had tended the coffee urns for
forty years as an affront and showing off. But the complaints were muted. However, when a Negro woman,
due to illness in the family or human frailty, failed to
show up on her Sunday, the comments were to the effect that you simply couldn't trust "them" to follow
through with their responsibility.

When the first Negro acolytes performed their ritualistic duties at the high altar and carried the cross in procession, there were audible gasps from some of the old-timers. But soon they became a fixture of our worship and the shock wore off.

How little and how shallow were our efforts toward integrating the congregation was evident at parish suppers. If Negroes came to these affairs they sat at tables by themselves. Few, however, came to parish social affairs and distressingly few of them turned up at Annual Meetings to approve the budget and vote for representatives of the congregation for Vestry positions. They were there but behaved like the second-class citizens whites had told them that they were for the last hundred years. But some were restive and told me by words and actions that they were willing and ready to take their responsibility as full members of the church.

It was obvious that an action group needed to be formed. As was pointed out in an earlier chapter, this took place and resulted in the election of Negroes to the Vestry, but it took five years. How it came about is interesting. One day I was talking over the problems of the minority-group people in the parish with my converted Jew and bewailing the fact that all the outward appearances of integration were meaningless when one honestly examined below the surface. An Annual Meeting was in the offing and once again I feared that either the same old tribal types would reelect themselves or at best an Uncle Tom would be put forward to safeguard the power structure. Hal agreed with me and made a few incisive comments. He asked if I minded if he went to work. I gave him the go-ahead, and waited. I didn't attend these meetings for fear of inhibiting the people, but Hal reported to me on his progress from time to time. His method was simplicity itself. He gathered together a group of young Caucasians and Negroes, single people and married couples. He spelled out to them the opportunity and explained the bylaws of the parish and what they could do to elect the best men, both white and black, to positions of responsibility at the Annual Meeting. It was a superb job. This group, having decided who they wanted from the old guard as well as the new, worked out a slate of candidates. They then took it upon themselves to acquaint others with the qualifications of the various people they had selected. In the meantime the old guard had decided among themselves who was fitted for the vast responsibilities of administering the parish affairs. The result was a large choice of candidates for the first time in history. As my ministry was to all the parish, I was in an interesting position to say the least, but in all honesty I was backing the Young Turks and most people knew it without my having to say a word publicly on the subject.

For the most part the old guard came to the Annual Meeting certain in their belief that all would go as usual and the same men would be elected. Imagine their alarm and outright anger when after the votes were counted the results showed that three brand-new men had been elected—two of them Negroes. They complained to me that there had been unfair politiking. I said I was aware of politiking but so far as I could see there was nothing dirty or underhanded, as they suggested. I also pointed out that in the new Vestry a majority of old-timers still outweighed the newcomers. This did not pacify them as they could correctly foresee that the day was not far off when new men, both black and white, would legally take over the management of the parish. Most of them took their defeat with more than a fair degree of sportsmanship. At this meeting only one man acted badly in public. He was overheard to declaim that now those sonsofbitches were getting on the Vestry he was through. The Negroes who heard this unlovely proclamation behaved with superb cool and politely pretended they hadn't heard a word.

Another aspect of parish integration which was fascinating to watch was that which took place in the Altar Guild. From the good old days of the father-builder of the magnificent edifice that is St. John's Church, the Altar Guild was more exclusive than the Colony Club in New York. Its membership was a status symbol. Naturally none of the elect were working women and so they were free to come on Friday mornings to do their work and to lunch after in the parish house. In the Episcopal Church the Altar Guild is responsible for cleaning the vessels used in Holy Communion, laundering altar linens and setting out the vestments for the weekday and Sunday services. Those who are admitted to the Altar Guild begin by polishing the brasses, the candlesticks, the altar rail, vases, etc. They then progress to linens and finally to the heights of knowing how to lay out the Eucharistic vestments for the priests. There was a very real hierarchy in the organization and one must say that they did their jobs well.

But time and death were cutting down the numbers who could work, and after a while at each meeting much time was spent bewailing the few who made up their membership. I waited and I waited. I didn't have to as I had authority to increase their membership any time I chose. But waiting seemed to be the right way. Finally the time came when they came to me and begged me to appoint some new members. I took a deep breath and then had a frank discussion with them about admitting nonwhite women to their ranks. I said I was unwilling to appoint any minority person to their group unless they were ready to accept new women in terms of full equality with themselves. There wasn't really much they would say to this but we did discuss it openly and frankly with the result that the new women I appointed were received with a fair degree of cordiality. The old guard were glad to have the extra hands and help. But there was a fly in the ointment. Most of the appointees were busy mothers of young children or working women and couldn't come to the Friday morning work and social sessions. They could come Sunday morning and set up the altar for the Eucharist and clean up after the service, but Friday mornings were out. But the work was done, linens washed and ironed, and the other minutiae attended to. While one can't say the ladies are soul sisters, at least they can and do work together in reasonable amity for the common good. From this association there are even signs of friendships developing outside the walls of the church building. But this is slow because the gap between minority and majority groups is slow, painfully slow, to close. Sort of like trying to watch a glacier move. One knows it is moving but the naked eye certainly cannot discern movement.

This seems to be how it works. The minority person in our society must take his place in the previously all-white Anglo-Saxon structures. He must learn the jargon as well as the tools of group action and interaction. Then as ability and humanity are shown and proved to be of worth and of equal value to that of the white majority the first signs of communion appear above the surface. It is easier for the Latin-American, and the American of Oriental heritage, to take his place beside the white than for the Negro American.

For some reason which I will leave to the psychiatrists to assess and analyze, the Negro is safe so long as he is in a servile role in American life. Once he dons a Brooks Brothers suit and his wife wears creations by Saks Fifth Avenue or I. Magnin, the threat to the Caucasian is measurable. Further, if the well-groomed and articulate Negro moves out of the Negro world in business or society, the average middle-class American is not only threatened but can easily become paranoid to one degree or another. Some hide it, but it is there whether visible or not. There seems to be economic fear, fear of social exposure that many say has sexual overtones. Certainly when a man says that he has nothing against Negroes but he doesn't want his daughter to marry one, there is real evidence that the fear lies very deep below the surface and much deeper than the words would imply.

The reverse English of this attitude is as complex and destructive as the one just described. I refer to the "do-gooder" and the liberal who blithely proclaim that they see no difference between black and white. Sometimes they go so far overboard that they lose all sense of objectivity. To them all Negroes are good, fine and noble; likewise, all whites except themselves and a few like them are bad, evil and akin to the Nazis. Quite obviously, not all Negroes are good. Some are bad, evil and dangerous to society. Some are ignorant, over-sensitive and self-righteous. This is also true of the Caucasian community.

No Caucasian can crawl into a Negro skull and know what it is to be a Negro American. One knows another person only in that the other person reveals something of himself. And there are deep hidden psychological areas which it is impossible for the Negro to reveal to a white person because he is unconscious that they exist. How can a white American know what it is to have been born into a Negro family set about with all the imposed and self-imposed taboos? How can the privileged Caucasian feel the inner turmoil of a Negro facing an all-white social or business situation? He can sense it, perhaps, but he cannot possibly know it in the way he knows his own insecurities. Can it be possible that the Negro smile hides fear of and hostility to the white American? Can the smile be the safest cover a black American can use in accommodating himself to difficult and humiliating circumstances? To answer any of these and other questions flatly Yes or No is to relapse into generalities, and most generalities in this very complex sociological and psychological problem are only partially true.

To the person who honestly wants social intercourse with Negroes, there is only one guideline and that is sensitivity, which one acquires only by making every mistake in the book. It also means that one must find Negroes who are willing to make the painful effort of dialogue in an atmosphere which at best is difficult for them. The Negro on his part must be willing to over-look the inevitable gaucheries of the white person seeking common grounds of interest and concern. While there are other things to talk about besides the race question, it is not a subject to be overlooked or avoided in Negro-white dialogue. Very often a frank discussion with understanding and humor on both sides results in a language each can begin to speak.

Both black and white have humanity in common, and that is important even though it is a cliché. For example, a Negro mother and a Caucasian mother have much in common through their children. Sickness, development and concern for their young form a common bond. Politics, business and local problems are certainly discussion openers for men. No matter how united white and black Americans may be in certain concerns and interests, the division of race soon enters the picture. It comes into the picture as soon as schools are mentioned, or housing or jobs. Negro children for the most part go to largely Negro schools. They live in either Negro areas or in lightly integrated sections of the American city. These stoppers to conversation must be dealt with if the Negro is going to take the Caucasian seriously. Sometimes this is painful, but these and other barriers to racial intercourse have to be faced if the meeting is to be anything but a superficial conversation which in the end does more harm than good.

To overidentify with the Negro is to lose the game. A white man or woman cannot turn into a Negro no matter how much he may want to (probably for all the wrong reasons). To maintain one's identity, whether Negro or Caucasian, is important. For in that way integrity can be born of the situation. We are well aware of the profound dislike of whites for the Negro who assumes all the outward characteristics of the

Caucasian. Similarly, the Negro is quick to assess the degree of phoniness of the white who adopts the language and mannerisms of the Negro. Both attitudes tend to interrupt dialogue and to dig even deeper the trench that separates. So you may say, be yourself in an interracial situation, remember who and what you are so that the wholeness and integrity of your person is honestly presented. This can do more good than talking about "whitey" and pretending to be that which you can't possibly be.

6

||||

SUBJECT–OBJECT SPLIT

One hot summer afternoon four years ago I was sitting on the front steps of the church surveying the view of autos, gas stations and casual foot traffic. An odd thing to do, but I was feeling uneasy, as if something important had been forgotten. The sick had been called on, the mail attended to, pastoral counseling appointments finished for the day. The physical plant of the church building and parish house looked cared for. In the office the parish secretary was finishing a long and tedious job. Parish activities had entered the summer doldrums. A time for reflection and planning for the year that lay ahead. Soon I would be in the woods and lakes and mountains of the Adirondacks in upper New York State. Yes, this was a time for planning and I wondered what to plan. The women's group had submitted a list of parish suppers and luncheons-with-speakers. Another guild was committed to sewing projects for the annual bazaar. The younger, newer apostolate had come to a standstill, having pulled their coup at the Annual Meeting. The Altar Guild had their duties and their new members. Even the Vestry as a whole was content, having recovered from their shocks earlier in the year. Even finances didn't look too discouraging. As rector of the parish I had every reason to feel satisfied. Progress was a measurable thing in terms of parish life and activity, even though small, and it looked as if the tide had begun to turn after so many years of defeatism and decay. Small, but real.

As I sat there I began to feel a very real depression. Was this what I was there for—to reconstruct the parish in the usually accepted understanding of what a parish is, i.e., organizations, congregations, services weekdays and Sundays? Were we there simply to revive a pattern? Which pattern was the approved one? Even the bishop had had kind words to say to me when I had seen him last. But I wasn't happy; something uneasy had entered my mind—a question the words of which hadn't become articulate. Something was missing. I couldn't say with any satisfaction that Rome wasn't built in a day. I felt as if I had been operating within a cocoon; an invisible web separated me and the parish from the rest of the Episcopal Church as well as from the city that swirled and hummed about us. What in the world was wrong with me? Had I lost my sense of direction in the day-to-day business of running a church and pastoral care for a congregation that lived in every section of our sprawling city? For the most part, the needs of the congregation were being met by me or the curate or the wonderful retired priest who had joined our staff on a part-time basis.

I began to think of my preaching. Sometimes I was good and sometimes bad, and sometimes I felt as if I were talking into the wind. Fine points of doctrine and the devotional life somehow weren't getting across. Sometimes the sermons were ill-prepared, yet even when they were painstakingly written out they had seemed to fall flat. I had contented myself by saying that I was tired, and in need of a holiday. But this afternoon the light of honest self-appraisal refused to let me gloss over the little worries and basic lack of satisfaction. Something creative and re-creative was missing from me and the parish life as a whole. The first hurdles had been overcome but the warning signs were everywhere for me to note. The midweek Lenten services, the discussion groups and other group activities were beginning to wilt visibly.

I had read many books on the renewal of the urban church. Exciting books by English and American priests who had done something extraordinary in terms of bringing new life into their parishes and the city. Roman Catholic priests in Paris had done exciting things. An English priest had instituted the house church. Paul Moore, now Suffragan Bishop of Washington, D.C., had written a wonderful book on the theology of the city parish. In thinking of these men and comparing their work with mine, I couldn't help but feel that some vital spark was missing from what the people of St. John's and I were doing.

All this time I had been smoking cigarettes and looking at the scene around me, scarcely conscious of its details. Focusing on the picture before my eyes, I saw individuals, in a sort of staggered procession, going along the avenue in cars and on bicycles and walking by on the sidewalk. People drove up to the gas station for a dollar's worth of gasoline. Children went to the coke dispenser and rode off on their bikes. Little children scampered across the church lawn and parking lot. Older men and women passed by carrying brown paper bags of groceries. There were not a few of the so-called single male drifters, so common in our cities, who venture out of skid row in search of a dollar or two which can buy them a room and a cheap bottle of wine. None came into the church and few even seemed aware that it was there with its special treasure of love for them. We had that locked up in our parish life and so sterilized that it would not infect even a mosquito.

A group of boys and girls under seven years of age came out of the Roman Catholic church across the street and went by chattering happily in Spanish.

What can St. John's, or any other church, mean in the lives of all these people? What are their special needs? Did the voice I heard calling for attention and help so many years ago come from any of them? What had I done with that plea except embalm it in my memory? Slowly it all began to take on meaning. I had to face the fact that in spite of our now orderly House of God, the church had been saying nothing, absolutely nothing, that had the slightest relevance to the lives of the people who lived near our sacred premises. Nor did it make any communication with the black ghetto, which began only a few blocks to the south of us. The people who made up the congregation on Sunday morning were as remote from the immediate needs of our adjacent areas as men from Mars. Even the Negro membership came from other sections of the city and the few whites or Negroes who lived within our legal parish boundaries were old-age pensioners who lived out their lives in seclusion and isolation that characterizes so many of the senior citizens who lay down the cudgels of life to await death and dissolution with patience and without hope.

A few days later I was paying a call on a mother who had had her share of this world's troubles. The home was a slum apartment within ten blocks of the church. I sat at an untidy kitchen table talking with her about the problems of a home without husband or father and inadequate public welfare funds to maintain anything but minimal existence. Three lively but unkempt children crowded around as we talked, sometimes listening solemnly, sometimes giggling at something the mother and I said. As I was talking I glanced over to a darker corner and saw what I at first thought was a dog under a blanket on the floor. I soon realized it was a two-year-old child. I said that I had thought she had only three children. "Oh, she said, that is Jimmy. He's queer." To make a long story short, I asked a number of questions which led me to understand that this "queer" child had never seen a doctor since he was born and that the mother regarded him as hopelessly retarded. She was fearful of mentioning him to the social worker and he was always hidden out of sight when the worker came to the house for fear that "he would be taken away."

It took a bit of persuading but finally I got her to agree to take the child to a private physician I knew for an examination. The result of the visit was the discovery that the child was congenitally deaf. With the assistance of the good doctor and a private foundation for the deaf, that child has learned to talk and lip-read, and is today a relatively normal, healthy child.

This was how the idea for a preventive medical facility for children was born in our parish. I told a number of people about the episode and the question was asked, "Why couldn't we do something for children?" The story of our clinic is not a success story, but perhaps it is a demonstration of the kind of thing a church can do when it looks about the world in which it finds itself. A very small demonstration at that.

It is a short story. A couple of men and women in the parish got interested in the idea. One man, who was recovering from a heart condition, made a survey of medical facilities in the general area of the church. He wrote a report, noting that there was a great need for a child health conference (a screening clinic) for children between the ages of two and six. For children up to two years of age the Well-Baby Clinics were doing a fine job. At the age of six the public school health program provided adequate medical screening and immunizations. In between, nothing seemed to exist to meet this need. The survey also showed that the number of pediatricians serving the great south central area of the city, largely the ghetto section of Los Angeles, numbered about nineteen for a population of nearly a half million persons.

The layman, Bob Thomas, put all his facts in a workmanlike document. Together we wrote up the proposal for a preventive pediatric clinic. Then we mailed it to everyone connected with public health, all the doctors we knew, as well as the president of the local Pediatric Society. For a while—a long while—we waited for someone to show an interest in our idea of getting volunteer doctors, nurses and trained lay people to begin a pilot project.

Then one day something happened which was to have far-reaching results—a phone call from a Dr. Holve, who asked for an appointment. When he met with Bob and me, we learned that he was president that year of the Pediatric Society. He had had a plan for a similar clinic but had thought that mobile units could be used. For a variety of reasons this had turned out to be impracticable. The idea of using the comparatively neutral atmosphere of a church struck him as sound. We soon called into our consultations Marian Clevenger, a dynamic matron in her middle years. Together we went to work. For nearly ten months we organized, and planned what equipment was needed. A gracious and professionally employed director of volunteers at a local hospital was co-opted to begin a training program for the good men and women of the parish who volunteered to serve. Volunteers were trained in the taking of social histories and rectal temperatures and in other related services. Experts in the fields of hearing and vision screening were obtained to teach our men and women how to operate an audiometer and the mysteries of the Snellen chart. Dr. Holve obtained the approval of the pediatric hierarchy, and a list of doctors who would volunteer their services on Saturday mornings was made up. Uniforms for the volunteers were obtained and one Saturday morning in July, 1964, we opened the doors of St. John's Well-Child Clinic.

Publicity and public relations efforts had been made to get our venture before the public and the various health agencies, private and public, in the city. Our test run was made up of children of parish families and we were pleased at the smoothness with which our medical and volunteer staffs operated and cooperated. The actual opening Saturday with honest-to-God appointments was a dud. Only five of the scheduled fifteen appeared. The next Saturday three came. The third Saturday none showed up. It was discouraging. I went about making the volunteers test their skills on one another and generally tried to belay the heavy gloom which had descended on our eager band of medical missionaries dedicated to bringing the light of health to a world which couldn't care less. A mother gave us the clue. "Why should I bring Johnny to your clinic when he is perfectly well?" she asked.

Preventive care was a product that was going to be hard to sell. And it was, for some months to come. As word got around to the social workers at the Bureau of Public Assistance our daily intake increased to about eight or ten children per clinic session. Some doctors dropped by the wayside, as did some volunteers, but for the most part they remained loyal to the effort. The need for better public relations was evident. So about six months after our rather dismal entry into the world of public health an open house was held to present our facility, its personnel and its stellar medical staff to the agency heads of the city. Everyone who was anyone was invited. And many came, including some of the public officials of the city. It was a great success and all expressed approval of what we had done. From that

day to this St. John's has never lacked a steady stream
of children going through our clinic doors.

A few facts may be interesting. The rooms used for
clinic purposes are Sunday school rooms which, otherwise, are used only once a week. Only one room had to
be taken out of general circulation; that was the room
chosen for the doctors' examining center with its examining tables, refrigerator for immunizing serums,
sterilizers, etc. The doctors do not wear white coats
but work in their shirt sleeves or sports shirts. The
nurses also do not appear in uniform. All parents or
guardians are welcomed with a cup of coffee as the
children are whisked away to have their weight,
height and temperatures recorded. If the child is very
young the mother goes with him through the various
stations and the final visit to the doctor for the thorough
physical examination. Armed with both a medical and
a social history previously obtained, the doctor spends
as much time with mother and child as he would in his
own office for a fee. He spends a lot of time telling the
mother what to expect from her child, what to look for,
what kinds of food will benefit him most; he also listens
to the problems of the child and the home. Primarily
the doctor teaches what he calls "soap-and-water medi-
cine." The purpose of the dialogue is to educate the
parent in the essentials of good health and medical
procedures. That this works and is well received is
shown by the fact that the rate of return visits is higher
than that of the public agencies and many parents call
in to find out when the annual visit to the clinic is due.

Money, curiously enough, has not been a problem
from the very beginning. The Vestry gave the clinic

the necessary malpractice insurance, as well as the refrigerator and new lights for the examination room. What with parish propaganda and a favorable newspaper article in the Los Angeles *Times,* donations have come in at a rate to keep the clinic in the black. The first year it cost nearly two thousand dollars to set the clinic in operation; the subsequent years it has cost about eight hundred dollars, including the insurance. A cheap price for the care of six hundred children a year. That figure does not include overhead such as staff salaries of the parish or utilities. The parish has decided that this is their responsibility and one they are happy to absorb for the time being.

A few general comments before leaving the story of our small venture into the field of preventive medical care of children. Not everyone in the parish thinks it is a good thing, although most do. The complaints are that the church shouldn't involve itself in this kind of work that doesn't bring in parishioners. It's true the clinic doesn't add names to the parish roll. The critics say that this sort of thing should be left to the county or city or someone else. We say in rebuttal that this is the kind of thing the church should do. Theologically it is giving a cup of water for Christ's sake, particularly when we ask for nothing in return. Again it would appear that the role of the church in today's urban civilization is that of the innovator. Where a need is not being met by the community it is the calling of the churches to learn how to meet this need and do it until someone or some organization comes along who can do it better and bigger than we. Our role is not to build empires. We must be ready to let go of our brain children when the time comes and look for new areas of need where the innovation of body and spirit are required, to point the way for others to follow. One day there won't be any St. John's Well-Child Clinic, but there will be, God willing, a fine medical facility in the area which will meet all the needs of children, both sick and well, in a way that our small operation cannot possibly do.

7

| | |

ENTER, REST AND PRAY

The average churchgoer has little or no idea what his minister does during the six days of the week following Sunday. They think that their pastor is a busy man on Sunday, what with services, sermons, Sunday school, and the coffee hour. For some reason they are reluctant to ask what he does the other six days. Some, I am sure, are convinced that having labored on the Lord's Day he rests, reads and prepares next Sunday's sermon, with a call or two on the sick in between his "busy" days. It is true, of course, that there are ministers who take advantage of this to sleep late and to indulge in a good deal of recreating and busy work to escape the daily grind of the parish office. These are the men who don't answer letters for months, read little and don't concern themselves with the life of their community other than membership in Rotary or Kiwanis. These are the men who appear to be organization men with (or without) round collars who are "good Joes" in the eyes of the average middle-class American. They usually have the good luck to have an excellent parish secretary who covers for them and makes them sound like the busiest men on earth.

But there are those who are in their church offices handling the mail, doing pastoral counseling, attending to the myriad chores of running an organization, as well as calling on the sick and shut-ins. Curiously enough, these are the men who answer mail and return telephone calls. They usually are active on the level of community life where it counts. They are members of welfare planning groups, coordinating councils, and other organizations which are attempting to do something concrete in the areas of human life which are neglected or ignored by the elected officials of any community.

The account of a typical day in the life of any minister would be interesting to examine. My own case, with a good office staff and dedicated assistants, is hardly typical of the one-man church, but it would certainly strike the average for the moderate-to-large city church.

The day usually begins at breakfast when I take out my appointment book to see what meetings and office appointments are scheduled for that day—and I wonder what I have forgotten to put in the book! In the car, driving to the church, I think of the various things that have to be done in addition to the scheduled appointments—things such as answering an accumulation of mail; studying the latest financial report of the Council of Churches; choosing someone to represent the parish at some diocesan meeting; and a number of other nagging things I have neglected for some time.

By the time I arrive at the office I am full of resolve to get my desk cleared and spend time on the things that really count, including visiting someone critically sick in the hospital. I arrive at the office and go over the mail, which is the usual collection of bills for the parish financial secretary, requests for transfer in and out of the parish, a stack of second-class junk mail which goes into the scrap basket unread.

As I am about to go to my office, the parish secretary reminds me that I had promised to write my piece for the parish newsletter today as it must get in the works today. I say, "Oh, yes," and start heading out the door. I get as far as the outside when she calls out that she has some telephone calls I must return. So I take three or four of the "while you were out" slips and note the names. One is from someone I never heard of; another is from a friend wanting to have lunch; and the other is from a frequently troubled parishioner—troubled with alcoholic fantasies.

I go to my office and sort out the various things on my desk in order of importance and prepare to pick up the phone when in walks the curate. He is relatively new, but capable and tactful of my vagaries. He has some things to discuss and I know they must be important. First, the schedule of services for the next month; then a projected program of adult study groups I wanted him to start; then there is the matter of replacing the Sunday school secretary who has just resigned. And by the way, he asks, have I written the letter of invitation to the people we hope to get on the next

weekend parish conference? I promise to write the letter
today. The buzzer rings and it is a telephone call for me
from someone who won't give her name. I take it and it
is a pleasant woman calling from the *Jewish Herald*
wanting to know if we wish to advertise in their
brotherhood edition. I thank her and say, "No," that
the budget for advertising is tight this year. I pick up
the phone to return the calls on the slips of paper and
dial the first number. I notice that Bob, the assistant, is
lingering at the door of my office with a questioning
look on his face. While the number is ringing, I ask him
if there is something else. He looks a bit embarrassed
and reminds me that I am due at a meeting of
the inner-city clergy in fifteen minutes. Had I forgotten? Yes, I had, and there isn't even a notation in my
date book, though I recall I had said I would be there.

I finish the rest of the telephone calls and dash out.
As I stop at the parish office to tell the secretary where
I will be, she tells me not to forget the finance meeting of the Church Federation at eleven-thirty. Another sin of omission so far as the date book is
concerned. As I get into the car I have a feeling of despair regarding all the untouched things on my desk
and wonder if I will ever get the newsletter piece or
the letter of invitation written, to say nothing of the unanswered mail. Damn, I think, and this is the day I
told the lady who comes in twice a week to take dictation to come in, because I had expected to have the
time to handle the mail this day. Well, perhaps the
afternoon will be quiet and we can do that!

I am almost on time for the inner-city clergy meeting
and realize with horror that the meeting is supposed
to include lunch. It is a good meeting and I hate to

leave when I must for the Church Federation. I murmur my regrets and leave in time to get to the finance
meeting, which turns out to be routine with most of
the important issues left for the next meeting.

On my return to the church, I determine it is high
time I went into the church for my daily devotions. So
I park the car and sneak into the church as if I were
going to an illicit assignation. I go in and sink to my
knees and begin the Lord's Prayer. I offer my all too
evident inadequacies to God and pray for the sick
and troubled by name. I am about to embark on a
petition to the Deity for help in determining the best
use of my time when there is a perfectly frightful crash
in the rear of the church. I look up just in time to see
two young boys running out the front door after
having upset the table with the tract rack on it. Fun
and games for them, but I must pick it up and sort out
the various pamphlets and put the thing in order again.
At least this time they didn't jimmy the alms box open,
nor did they scribble obscenities in the guest book!

My prayer life shattered, I enter the office area where
more telephone messages await me as well as an unexpected appointment. A woman wants to talk with me
about the details of her daughter's wedding. I give a de-
spairing look at the secretary and invite the woman to
come into my office. It seems that she wants her daughter's wedding to be "a bash." Music, soloists, candles
down the aisle. Yes, it will be a big wedding with four
or five hundred guests. No, she isn't a member of the
Episcopal Church nor is her daughter or prospective
son-in-law—"But your church is so pretty I thought it
would be nice." In other words, I think, you just want
a nice hall for your wedding. I explain to her that we

simply don't have weddings in our parish church just because it is a pretty place but, rather, on the basis of religious convictions. Does either she or her daughter go to a church? Well, no, she says, but she thinks a church wedding is a nice thing. I agree and suggest that she try a big downtown church, which might be agreeable to her plans. She leaves, and I wonder if I have done the right thing.

By this time the clock says half-past three and I must either do my dictation or put it off for another three days. I call in Mrs. C., the secretary, and we begin to take care of the pile. A letter to a former parishioner who wants to know what happened to old Mrs. F. Another to a clergyman in another state asking him to please forward the transfer of a parishioner. The others are fairly routine so we finish quickly. Then out of sheer desperation I proceed to dictate the letter I promised, inviting people to the conference weekend, and my "message" for the newsletter. As Mrs. C. picks up the correspondence and prepares to go back to her typewriter she says she doesn't think she can finish before she has to leave but will come in tomorrow. I thank her and pick up the phone to return the calls which have accumulated into a threatening pile on my desk.

"Reverend, may I speak to you for a minute?" It is a seedy-looking character. I hear his story even though I know it before he starts. He is out of work, isn't eligible for welfare and needs money for carfare as well as for food because he hasn't eaten for two days. I give him a dollar and wish him well, knowing that it is a waste of money but hoping for the best. I am too harassed and pressed for time to do more; I know I should have spent more time with him.

At half-past five I have completed all the telephone
calls and most of the pressing things on my desk and
get ready to go home for an early supper, as I have confirmation class in the early evening. I go into the church
again for a moment of quiet but find that someone has
lighted every vigil light in sight and there are burnt
matches all over the church. I call Bob, the assistant,
and ask him to take care of it while I rush home for
supper, stopping on the way at the hospital where a
man is in the intensive-care unit recovering from heart
surgery. He is glad to see me and grateful for the prayer
offered for him.

Home for a short time for a brief meeting with my
wife and family before returning to the church. The
confirmation class is restless and I wonder, probably
correctly, if I am repeating last week's lesson or
whether I am confusing them as I undertake to explain
to them the meaning of myth in terms of Christian
terminology. From the questions I get and from the
shock of one of them I gather I have really done a bad
job. So I begin all over again, with better luck the second time. We finish the session with questions and discussions and have a lively debate on issues arising from
the problems of the conflict between the Negro and
Caucasian communities. Weary as I am at that point,
I don't want to end the first sign of life, and the discussion continues with great good humor as well as reality
between the Negro and white members of the class.
While it has nothing to do with the content I tried so
hard to give them, I feel that this is far more worth-
while than theological niceties. Finally, having resolved
little but having opened vast areas of understanding,
we close the session. As I get into my car I hear a

white couple and a Negro couple from the class decide to go on to some place for coffee. In some strange way I feel that while I had little to do with this it is a nice reward at the end of a frustrating and strangely tiring day.

I get home, take off my coat and collar and dive into the icebox for a beer. My wife discusses her day and its various complexities and I tell her about the various doings of my day. So the day ends with putting the dog out for his final run and switching off the lights. I note with dismay that it is midnight when I turn out the light by my bed, and tomorrow is another day. Please God, I say, as I drift off to sleep, it will be more effective than today.

8

| | | |

CHRISTIAN UNITY
COMES HARD

An aspect of contemporary Christian parish concern is
that of the movements toward unity that all go under
the head of ecumenism. It may be on the official and
somewhat sterile agenda of a Council of Churches,
cluster ministries, or unofficial or *sub rosa* work and dialogue with the Church of Rome. I cannot put a finger
on when exactly in my personal history the passionate
desire for Christian union and reunion entered my
soul; it remains there as a constant source of both in-
spiration and despair. Whenever it did happen, it
changed my whole concept of the life and work of a
minister in the Episcopal Church. No longer was I particularly proud of the differences which separate Episcopalians from our Protestant brothers or our Roman
Catholic and Orthodox brothers. The carefully nur-
tured apologia for the Church of England and the

Anglican Communion suddenly became excuses, and poor ones, for not seeking and searching out the realities that unite us all. It brought a certain freedom in my conversations with Protestants and Catholics that hadn't existed before. No longer did I have to feel superior because of our ecclesiastical order, sacraments and liturgy when meeting with other Protestant ministers; no longer did I feel it necessary to emphasize the catholicity of the Anglican Communion with Roman Catholics.

Perhaps it was the six months taken off from parish duties, during which I took a course in ecumenics at our seminary in Cambridge, Massachusetts; but more likely it was the fellowship I had during that same period with Catholic priests and Protestant ministers and laymen at Harvard Divinity School. In any case, it was about that time and probably as a result of the confrontations in Cambridge that the steel of ecumenism entered my soul. Also it was the Pontificate of Pope John XXIII which undoubtedly had a great deal to do with my conversion to the whole idea of Christian reunion. Certainly upon my return to Los Angeles and my duties as rector of St. John's ecumenism was much on my mind.

Shortly after I came back from that wellspring of intellectual and theological ferment to be found in and around Harvard University, I was asked to become a board member of the local Council of Churches. I accepted this honor and opportunity eagerly. Here was one place to begin. Frustration set in quickly. It wasn't too long before I decided that the Church Federation is probably the last place to find genuine ecumenical commitment.

A typical board meeting goes something like this. The meetings are always luncheon affairs so there is usually a bit of congenial confusion prior to the business meeting. The president introduces new members and guests. Once in a while we go through that hideous routine of standing up and telling our name, denomination and parish. The Executive Secretary then calls on the various department heads to make their reports. This can be dreary, especially when the so-called Christian education released-time people get up and tell how many children and volunteer teachers are involved. Then they usually tell of the latest money-making project to boost the dwindling financial support of the operation.

I should have preceded this with a description of the *mise en scène*. These meetings of the Council of Churches take place in the most improbable former residence imaginable, on Adams Boulevard not too far from St. John's. It is sort of a Wagnerian version of a Charles Addams house replete with a two-story dry waterfall in one area and a pipe organ dominating another. The dining room where these ecumenical luncheons take place has dark, ornate mahogany paneling and a fireplace enlivened with hand-painted scenic panels above the wainscoting. This may possibly have depressed the ecumenical fervor of the participants in the monthly board meetings and so account for the general dreariness of these affairs.

Worthiness is the watchword of the Council of Churches meetings. There is a sort of forced heartiness about the whole thing which only underlines how far separated the brethren are after God knows how many years of meeting and working together. The word "ecumenical" is tossed about from time to time, but hardly taken seriously. It is a group of men and women from various Protestant churches who view with some suspicion the Episcopalians and politely refrain from any overt or covert attempt to include Roman Catholics or Orthodox ministers or laity in their fellowship. Once when a Roman Catholic priest, who happened to be head of a Council of Churches in a nearby area, ventured into this fellowship, they made such a fuss about him he never returned. One cannot blame him.

The meeting usually concludes with the report of the treasurer which makes one wonder if all this money couldn't be better used elsewhere. Apparently, many churches have decided that their time and treasure can be better spent because the figures indicate a declining support and membership.

Not all is wasted at these affairs because one can and does meet interesting and dedicated men from other denominations. It was out of this group of people that a new approach to area problems was born, thanks to the urban executives of the Episcopal, Presbyterian and Methodist churches. Someone had the idea that churches in a given area should work together in the whole area of community needs. This would give the relatively weak efforts of the various individual churches support and allow the opportunity for combined and coordinated programs to take place. Waste and duplicated efforts would be eliminated and together these churches might become a vital part of the community enterprise.

This is how the idea of the Greater University Parish was conceived. Under the dynamic leadership of a Presbyterian minister, Bob Ryland, we began meeting together for breakfast and a discussion every Friday morning at seven thirty at St. John's Church. Our common ground was that we had churches in the general area around the university. We were Negro, Korean, Japanese and Caucasian; we were Methodist, Presbyterian, Baptist, Lutheran, Episcopalian and a few other denominations. Later we were joined by a couple of Roman Catholic nuns to round out the ecumenical picture. Another thing we had in common, besides our central-city area, was our Christianity, but curiously enough the latter has never been a strong binding force. The spirit of ecumenism hasn't really struck this grass-roots area of Christianity. So far as the Protestant brands are concerned, ecumenism means Protestants working together on common projects for the benefit of the community. When confronted by some ecclesiastical or theological issue, everyone gets very polite or falls silent. So from the standpoint of genuine ecumenical encounter the Greater University Parish is nothing to boast about, but we have some useful projects started. The seeds are there in the soil and any day now the sprouts may begin to appear.

Perhaps most important of all is that over the two-year period that G.U.P. has been going we got to know one another better as people. We have, with the help of the denominational bodies, operated a walk-in social service center on nearby Jefferson Boulevard. We, together with a VISTA team under the direction of an Episcopal worker priest, ran a camping program for hundreds of slum children one summer. One Fourth of July we had a Freedom Fair on the playground of a neighboring Roman Catholic parochial school.

Recognizing that a group of clergymen are not exactly the right people to run such an organization, the last year we have made a real attempt to include laity from the various churches represented. Unhappily, the laity are so used to having their ministers speak for them that they haven't yet got the idea that their role in both their individual churches and in the Greater University Parish is far more important than that of their respective ministers. When that day comes the organization will really get going and, like it or not, the clergy will have to take a back seat.

The failure of the churches to recognize the vital function of the laity is all too evident when you get a group of clergy and laymen from various denominations together to work out a common purpose. The ecclesiastical straight-jacket of the Episcopalians, the theological weakness of the Methodists, the political structure of the Presbyterians and Lutherans, and the lack of church structure of the others also contribute to the general confusion that can occur when churchmen of differing stripes get together. All one can say is that there is a general aura of good will, but more often than not this is offset by the mutual ignorance of the individual traditions and faith positions, and even of one's own denominational stand.

One of our members has tried time and time again to get the ministers to study the documents of the ongoing Consultations on Church Union currently being undertaken by a number of the major Protestant denominations. The general reaction has been lukewarm and to date no one has taken the suggestion seriously. Yet it can be said with some certainty that until the various separated churches come together for the common or uncommon good of a community on the

basis of a strong foundation of faith, their efforts in any
direction will be puny. This means that the blood-
and-guts center of Christianity must be rediscovered as
a common denominator and that the ancient evils of
separatism and self-glorification must be put aside
with a real degree of humility. Without a real effort to
find that which unites all Christians, all efforts at grass-
roots ecumenism will be doomed to do-goodism.

The real tragedy of the Council of Churches is that
members are promoting slogans which were outdated
before World War II. In order to gain a little publicity
they take some rather pompous stands against public
and private morality; occasionally they will embrace
a liberal cause for the sake of being liberal rather than
having concern for the issue involved. There are excep-
tions to every generalization and our bias arises from a
local situation which may not represent a true picture of
the Councils of Churches everywhere. I well recall my
initiation to the local Church Federation in Massachusetts nearly twenty years ago. Each meeting was devoted to the question of how best to get the liquor stores
off the main street. Apparently to those reverend gentlemen it would be preferable to have them hidden in
back alleys where juveniles could more easily obtain
alcoholic beverages from unscrupulous storeowners. It
appeared that they felt the town was presenting a bad
image by having purveyors of demon rum on its main
street. Not much changes in spite of the years. Only
recently there was a national commotion about a report allegedly prepared for the National Council of
Churches which disclosed the rather sophisticated
recommendation that young people should be allowed
to drink at the age of eighteen and generally recom-
mended a more relaxed attitude toward drinking. Im-

mediately the fur began to fly and public statements were made by spokesmen of local and national Councils of Churches denying any responsibility for such a loose proposal. The Puritan ethic and the spirit of Carrie Nation die hard!

The failure of the Council of Churches to promote Christian unity in no way invalidates the idea that an ecumenical organization of some sort is necessary. Until such time as there is a radical change in the Council of Churches, or it is buried, there will continue to arise groups of Christians who believe that God is calling Christians to a unity of thought, purpose and, ultimately, even, organization. We need to know one another better; we need to share authentic information about the Christian faith and the historical present; we must learn to pool our resources to meet the human agony of a world and a nation in crisis.

With the rise of a genuine conservative movement within the United States, it is obvious that those churches which promote the conservative cause will flourish. The main-line liberal Christian institutions are going to lose both support and treasure as the wave of reaction grows. Unity will then be a practical necessity, but whether or not the Council of Churches mentality will read the handwriting on the wall, one cannot foretell. Perhaps members will find it more convenient to bend before the wave of the future if support for their crumbling institutions is forthcoming from the New Right. It will be a time when the men will be separated from the boys, and the men will have a pretty tough time of it until the wave recedes.

In viewing the various ecumenical relationships, it is a bit discouraging that for the most part the meetings that take place have a lot less to do with the

Christian faith than they do with budgets and inter-church cooperation in various community projects and organizations. While our little cluster offers real hope and ecumenical potential, I can state quite honestly that the only genuine ecumenical experiences and relationships I have had in the past ten years have been with some of our Roman Catholic friends. Having emerged from the strictures of the Council of Trent with the explosive action of Vatican Council II, there are many, many priests, brothers and nuns who are eager for meetings with their long-estranged Christian brothers and sisters of the separated churches.

Having been denied fellowship with their fellow Christians for so many centuries, the Roman clergy are eager and ready to discuss any and all matters theological. They are in many cases far better informed than the non-Roman clergy in current religious and philosophical reading. Their disappointment can be profound when they find that the genial Protestant minister can barely offer his hand in friendship, let alone his heart in Christ's name.

Genuine ecumenical work cannot be done, nor can any kind of Christian perspective be gained in terms of our cultural, social and economic turmoil, unless Protestants get off their high horses and meet Roman Catholics as equals, and many times as their superiors, in their understanding of the faith and in the religious and academic spheres. One can only hope that in the months and years ahead we may take advantage of the new spirit of desire where the climate will create new bonds of brotherhood and companionship in the name of the One we all profess to serve.

9

| | | |

VOICES IN THE NIGHT

"No home, condemned by man as a bastard. No right to go to church. Pray for me." These were the words I found scribbled one morning in the guest book which resides near the front door of the church. These phrases haunt me today as I write them down again. Who wrote them? In my mind's eye I see a man in ragged clothes with fierce and desperate eyes. He must have come into the church looking for help and, finding none, left with this valedictory or curse at the indifference to hunger and cold only a beautiful building can have. Concrete, marble, mosaic and gilt have little to offer a desperate man. In all probability the church had been left open longer than usual and the offices were closed.

Whoever wrote in the guest book, his is a voice that

is seldom made articulate—the voice of frustrated and desperate men and women who haunt our city streets, having come looking for work, help and guidance in a world which today recognizes only skills and accomplishment as worthy of concern. The flotsam humanity adrift on the surface of our urban life is swept aside by the currents of technology and progress which mark the mainstream of American life. Yet these are people, human lives which once had vigor, hope and faith in a future. Now they prowl the streets, sleep in parks, under railroad bridges and occasionally in the rescue missions in the tenderloin district. No longer are they seeking anything concrete in the way of a life, but for the most part they are looking for the oblivion to be found in a bottle of wine. Only occasionally do they surface in anger like the unknown author of the words of desperation found in the guest book.

But in the city this is only one of the voices a pastor hears in the night. Most often the voice comes over the telephone. A mother whose child has failed to come home. A husband whose wife is out with another man. The whole gamut of human crisis and failure cry out in the nighttime for help to the minister, the police or anyone who might care.

I remember vividly one occasion when the telephone rang at about two in the morning. The caller was a husband whose wife was dying in the hospital. He said he couldn't rouse his priest and he wanted a minister for his wife. I threw on my clothes, grabbed my Prayer Book and stopped at the church for the oil for the last anointing. I found the hospital, one of the older ones at that time, which medical progress had passed by. The room was crowded with relatives who, crying and sobbing, were already behaving as if the poor woman were dead. Death is rarely attractive but this was indecent. I went over to the bed and talked with the patient, who was conscious and very fearful. One feels so inadequate at times like this.

I took her thin hand in mine and began to say the "Our Father" quietly; soon she joined me as did the various relatives around the bedside. I then gave her the absolution and went right on into the commendaion for the dying. She was too ill to receive the sacrament, so I anointed her. The last words of the commendation contain this: "May thy rest be this day in peace, and thy dwelling-place in the the Paradise of God." To my great surprise she lost her fearful look and squeezed my hand. She closed her eyes and murmured the word "Paradise" and without any further sound crossed that barrier we call death. This was a typical experience of an inner-city priest. I had never heard of these people before the telephone call and never heard of them after.

Another time the early morning call came from the young husband. He had taken his wife to the hospital in labor with her first child. It was a difficult labor and he was fearful. Would I come? When I arrived at the waiting room, I found the father-to-be smoking one cigarette after another, sitting in absolute dejection. He told me of the complication and his fears that his wife would die. He said there had been doubt if she could even conceive a child, but the miracle had happened. I had seen them in church Sunday after Sunday during the pregnancy and two happier or thankful people would have been hard to find.

Now their hopes were threatened and he feared

not only the loss of the hoped-for baby but the very life of the mother herself. As we sat there in that waiting room during those long hours he told me of their courtship, the difficulties they had encountered in their short marriage and the joy of their relationship. Time went by slowly. At one point I went out and got us each a cup of coffee from a dispenser downstairs. Toward the first light the young man fell into a troubled sleep and I began to feel sleepy too as I went through some rather ancient *Reader's Digests*. Around six o'clock the doctor came down, woke up the husband with the overwhelming good news that a baby boy had been born and the mother was fine. Only minor surgical intervention had been necessary at the last and the complications had been minor after all.

George heard the news wooden-faced until the doctor left, when he smiled faintly and then tears of joy flooded his face. I decided then that the best therapy for him would be a good breakfast, so I persuaded him to go along with me. After a hearty meal I left him once more at the hospital and went on to the church office for a day which promised to be one of routine appointments. But there was joy in my heart as I thought of the loving reunion of the young couple who had come for a brief time under the shadow of death only to be delivered from it with a new life to love and care for.

Another night the voice over the phone said, "Father, I must make my confession. It can't wait." I took the address and dressed as quickly as possible. Arriving at the spot designated, I thought there must have been some mistake because it was a bar. Nonetheless I went in and sure enough a man came up to me a bit unsteadily and identified himself as the caller. Would I have a drink with him? I got myself a beer and sat at his table while he had one he hardly needed. As we sat there he unfolded a tale of a life so wasted and so futile it made my heart ache. Broken marriages and relationships and oft-changed jobs had marked his adult life. He felt he had come to the end of the road and there was no way out but what he called "the long sleep." I listened for a long time before I began to talk to him. I told him that he could begin again and there was help for him—both medical, spiritual and practical —if he chose to live. He asked me how he could ever make amends for all the people he had hurt, the people who had loaned him money and got him jobs he promptly lost. His children were ashamed of him and refused to see him when he called; his parents had escaped to the Nirvana of a retirement community in a distant part of the country. I tried to tell him that if he made the choice and implemented it with an effort to rehabilitate himself he would not only have the support and love of his family but also his friends.

I thought I was eloquent and even persuasive. He listened quietly and was silent for a long time after I stopped talking. Finally he looked up and said, "I'm sorry, Father, I just don't believe I can do it. Thanks anyhow, for trying. Go home and get a good night's sleep. Say a prayer for me." Realizing finally that there was nothing more I could do, I asked him to come and see me in the morning and we could talk some more. He thanked me, said he would, and took my card.

All day I waited for him to come or telephone, but that was the last I ever heard of him except a brief notice in the newspaper a day or two later saying that the body of a man hit and killed by a truck had been identified. It was my friend in the bar. I had another failure to offer up to God in prayer.

There are times when I wonder about what our fathers referred to as "divine providence." Does God really care? If so, why the suffering and waste in the death of a child? The best answer I have is that it simply isn't God's will that an innocent child die. The processes of creation include in them decay, disease and death; they are quite impersonal and impartial when and where they strike. In another age it was thought that the sin of the child or the parents was responsible. But today that is unthinkable in terms of a universal God whose heart is love. All one can say is that a particular disease strikes as part of the never-ending pattern of the battle for survival of man and beast. Man's valiant fight against disease is his answer, angry sometimes, to the enemies of human growth and life.

These thoughts and others I have had as I watched at the deathbed of a child. One comes to mind with singular poignancy. Kurt was one of two little boys of a broken marriage. He was twelve years old and was being brought up by his aunt, who lived near the rectory. He was a bright, dark-eyed boy. One winter we noticed that he didn't want to play ball with the other children in the neighborhood. Taken to the hospital for a medical answer to his lassitude it was discovered that he was suffering from leukemia. While he was never officially told, he was bright enough to figure out his trouble. But with a deep understanding of adult foibles he kept his knowledge to himself and only told me toward the end of his life. The battle for his life

went on for two years. Transfusions, bed rest, chemo-
therapy and all the rest of it were tried by the doctors
battling on the verge of discovery of a cure for this
killer. He had several periods of remission.

During the progress of the disease I got to know this
child well. He was confirmed by the bishop during
one of his up periods and received the sacrament regularly from me. He was very mature in his acceptance
of Christianity and didn't cling to the symbols of faith
like a crutch, but used the whole cloth of his religion
to give him acceptance to the mysterious forces which
were going to bring him to death. I never saw him cry
even though he was very discouraged as things went
from bad to worse.

He always had a cheery smile for visitors and they
usually went away more helped than having helped.
His death came quickly after a period of remission
faded. I was called to the hospital when he was rushed
there after a severe hemorrhage. He was kept waiting
in an emergency room interminably until the doctor
could be found to come to see him. He was given mas-
sive tranfusions by his father and myself, but even these
efforts were of no avail. He was returned to his home
where he died the next day, quietly, as the sun was going down—without a murmur, with his estranged
parents at the bedside.

We don't know why Kurt died before he had a
chance to become a man. We know the disease and
how it operates. But the why must remain unanswered
while we on this side of life can only see through the
glass darkly.

10

||||

NEW ALTAR—SAME GOD

The marvelous adaptability of the human being has been at no time and no place better demonstrated than in this century of unbelievable change. One sees in the transcontinental jets elderly women whose first ideas of travel were the buggy and the iron horse. These same women who began housekeeping by stoking a coal or wood stove, happily go home, take a piece of frozen food from the freezer and cook it on a gas stove. In the evenings they sit before their television sets watching "Gunsmoke" or "Peyton Place."

The American has not only accepted change as part of the fuller life but has embraced it with enthusiasm as each new development has taken place in his life.

Curiously enough, while all the world has changed and the way in which we live has undergone radical and sometimes violent change, the churches have re-

mained static and immovable in their way of worship
until very recently. And if there is any one single thing
a minister can do to raise the hackles of his congregation it is to change the order of the worship service.
Even a small change can start off a chain reaction of
controversy which is capable of reproducing the con-
vulsions which followed the European and English
Reformations.

In the Protestant, Roman Catholic and Episcopal
Churches, worshipers have been doing the same things,
saying the same things, and hearing the same things in
the same way since the sixteenth and seventeenth centuries. Until very recently the Roman Mass was in Latin
and a priest varied the established pattern of worship
at the risk of excommunication or at least a severe
reprimand from his bishop. No less rigid has been the
order of worship in the Protestant and free churches.
However, Vatican Council II and the whole spirit of
renewal throughout Christendom are bringing change
to the formerly immutable forms of worship.

It is necessary to give a bit of historical background
before telling how liturgical renewal comes to the
Church. The denominations which came out of the
birth pangs of the sixteenth century restored the bread
and wine of Communion to the lay people. Further,
they all revised their liturgies and put them in the common tongue in the various countries. Basically the
liturgy of the Communion remained what it was
minus some of the funguslike accretions which had
grown upon it. If one compares the liturgies of the re-
formed churches one is struck by the similarity of the
elements present in them as well as in the Roman
Catholic Mass.

Of all the liturgies to come out of the Reformation, the one of greatest beauty of language and simplicity of expression was that of the Church of England. Even today one hears the sixteenth-century English of Archbishop Cranmer and is mesmerized by the sheer beauty of its words and the music that is the language of Shakespeare. Lacking nothing in the essentials of the Orthodox or Catholic Churches, the Anglican Eucharist has shone like a jewel for the more than four centuries it has been used by the Church of England and its daughter churches around the world, including the Episcopal Church in the U.S.A.

However, in spite of its beauty, the Episcopal liturgy is aging and has become somewhat archaic. But even more archaic than the language of the Holy Communion is the manner in which it is celebrated. Facing the altar, the priest, separated from the people by choir and many steps, says or sings in dulcet tones the ancient phrases and reads the Bible lections from the King James Version. The people, unable to participate except in the stated places, can easily be lulled into a sort of trance which soothes the mind and induces a general sense of well-being. "Decency" and "order" are the two words which govern the general tone of the service. Decency and order—not rapture and ecstatic union.

As practiced in Anglican churches from Bombay to London to Toronto to Des Moines to San Francisco, the liturgy varies little. But the language is no longer the language of the people and the actions of the priests have little or nothing to do with congregational response. A museum piece, but hardly one that reaches the contemporary mind and heart. There is more truth than Episcopalians like in the crack made by a Roman priest to an Episcopal priest after Vatican Council II cleared the way for putting the Roman Mass into the language of the people. He said, "Now we are putting our Mass in English; when are you?"

But renewal of the basic Christian liturgy is more than language and vestments. It is finding once again the vital core of the action of priest and people as together they offer the bread and wine and receive back the food they consider holy. The real renewal movement began with the Benedictine monks at Maria Lach in Germany in the 1920's. It was taken up by individual daring priests in France. It spread to the Protestant churches in Europe and across the seas to the United States and elsewhere. To make the fundamental Christian reality and mystery known and lived was the basic intent. Old ways were discarded even when the words remained the same. Holy tables in or near the people replaced altars far removed from congregations. Lay people began to read the Epistle lesson, to present the bread and wine of Communion to the clergy. In some areas of the Anglican Communion lay persons administered the cup at the Holy Communion.

While all this may seem a change which had little effect except within the walls of the church, strange things began to happen. In France, priests joined labor unions and took factory jobs, saying Mass often at the lunch break. Other priests, especially trained, went in ordinary civilian clothes to discuss existentialist philosophy versus Christianity with the café intellectuals in Paris. An Anglican priest in Leeds, England, began the house church movement in which instruction classes, Bible study and services of Holy Communion at kitchen tables in the homes of workers took place, replacing the sterile church services people stayed away from.

As the various churches became renewed, or began the process, a curious phenomenon could be observed. The Church began to be involved in the problems of people in today's world. It began to take social action seriously. Thanksgiving and Christmas baskets to the poor were replaced by priests and Christian people doing things in the community about wages, housing, civil rights and political questions which had moral implications. At the same time, old barriers began to break down between Christian bodies. Informal and formal conversations took place between clergy of differing persuasions; joint action programs for various reform measures in communities sprang up. People asked, "What has happened to our church?" Even before Vatican Council II this was happening. However, Vatican II forever opened the sluice gate which in time, maybe a long time, will join the rich stream of Latin Christianity and the separated churches back into one body to do Christ's work on this planet. Hierarchies cannot stop this onrush of flood waters though retrograde coffer dams may slow it up from time to time. History is forcing the renewal of Christians.

The pious image of American Protestantism and the sacrosanct quality of Roman Catholicism is disappearing bit by bit. As the Church loses its self-righteousness and its sense of propriety it loses support from those who represent the *status quo*, but it becomes more the image of its Creator in the world. By the end of this century the Church may well lose much property and real wealth. It may have far fewer members, fewer churches and institutions, but it will become the community of love and work it was in the days of its youth, with vigor to fight and defeat the Goliaths of this world.

Renewal, however, cannot stop with worship and social action. It must reach down into the very structures of the Church's own life. Its inner life must be re-examined and simplified. The age-old anachronisms of the bishops, archbishops, superintendents and presbyteries must be streamlined if the churches are to move effectively in an age in which speed is measured in terms of light rather than a coach-and-four.

Ambivalence in a world which scientifically measures truth and works can no longer be excused. The churches with one foot in Wall Street and the other in the sanctuary must choose. No longer can they bless the body politic or the management class uncritically. If the Church in some way represents a moral conscience that is of God, then it can no longer wink at evil in the established order of things in these United States. The churches south of the Mason-Dixon Line cannot in conscience maintain two sets of church buildings, one for Negroes and one for whites. The Church, wherever it finds itself, cannot be the Church and derive support from institutions which violate the cardinal law of love. It is a time for decisions, and hard ones.

Renewal and reform must go from bishops and their minions and committees and departments right on down to the smallest parish and mission. This will not be easy because the Church has its own laws, and every parish has its bylaws. Rome has it easier with one set of canon law for all, but reform of Roman canon law won't be easy either.

The Church in its official attitudes and acts is an

anachronism in today's society. It has a museum quality which is evocative and has a certain charm, but on the whole it is hardly relevant to the lives of people living in a technological world with problems undreamed of in the days of its influence and opulence.

The parish church cannot any longer wait for the elephantine rebirth of the Church if it is to survive and flourish in terms of usefulness and as the fountainhead of love from which the thirsty world can drink. This is why one sees signs of new life in parish churches all over the United States as well as in other parts of the world. Dialogue between various Christian groups takes place with or without the permission of the hierarchies. Under advanced leadership one sees Catholics, Episcopalians and Protestants band together to do the work that needs to be done in the slums of Kansas City, New York and other metropolitan centers. One doesn't have to go far to see an Episcopal priest celebrate the Eucharist at a Roman Catholic altar. Group Bible study in interfaith settings is becoming commonplace. Work programs for delinquents, jointly undertaken by Protestants and Catholics on an informal or formal basis, are developing. No longer do Christians try to bring the outcast into his particular denomination or communion. Scalp-hunting is no longer *de rigueur* among the growing band of Christians who are united in action and love, though separated by centuries of bitterness and theological statements which no longer have relevance.

This is the atmosphere of rebirth that is beginning to take root and spread wherever there are Christians in spite of the road blocks that are set up by reactionary or unthinking Christians who still make up the majority of American Christianity.

Revolutions come as the result of the dissatisfaction of a minority who push for reform within a human structure in which the structure itself has become more important to the rulers than the human ends that shaped it originally. This is true of nations, and it is true of the Church. Usually the occasion for the outbreak of revolution is less important than the volcanic forces deep underneath the surface. It is a new wisp of smoke coming from Vesuvius; the accidental firing on Fort Sumter; the murder of an Austrian archduke.

At St. John's our revolution began in a very simple way. Having read and observed some of the liturgical reforms within our Communion as well as the Roman Communion both pre- and post-Vatican Council II, a group of interested and dedicated men and women began to pressure me to have a free-standing altar. I had long desired this but had hesitated, fearing a strong reaction on the part of the more conservative members of the congregation.

After what we all thought adequate preparation by written and spoken word, we began in January, 1967, to prepare for this liturgical innovation. A very gifted layman began working on designs while the rest of us worked out the logistics. A plan developed which involved taking out the first five pews in the front and turning transept pews to face in toward the center aisle. While much work was done in advance, nothing was done in the church proper until the first week in Lent, when about thirty men and women gathered every night, unscrewing pews and putting in place a cir-

cular dais sixteen feet in diameter. A moving company
put the discarded pews in what might have been a bel-
fry. A man came in to lay the vinyl tile on the dais
while others refinished the newly exposed floor. Then
the new holy table was placed in the center of the dais,
flanked by two huge brass candlesticks resurrected
from the basement. The artist created a masterpiece
in the holy table. It is modern yet reminiscent of the
twelfth-century artifacts in the church. Saturday, late
in the day, all was in readiness. So far as the liturgy
itself was concerned, nothing was to be changed
from the usual formula of Matins and Eucharist. The
new liturgy had not been authorized at that time.
The only difference would be the new holy table
with the officiating ministers behind it facing the people; same words, same actions. We carefully rehearsed
so that the movement of the liturgy would be smooth.

That Sunday we had more people than usual in
church—perhaps because of the innovations, perhaps
because it was the first Sunday in Lent. Those who had
worked so hard to create the beautiful new altar arrangement were tense, fearing a radical reaction against
it. I myself was nervous, feeling the various tensions.

The service went beautifully in every respect and
afterward the majority came up to those of us who
had been involved in the work to congratulate us.
Many said they had heard the service for the first
time and that the closeness of the clergy to the congregation made them feel a part of the Eucharist. Some
held their judgment until they got used to it. Among
a small minority, however, the reactions against were
surprisingly violent. We had desecrated the church,
violated the artistic integrity of the building and had

created a monstrosity which made worship difficult for them.

In retrospect, I cannot blame the diehards or rather the reactionaries to liturgical renewal. They had been raised in the Episcopal Church and had for the most part known nothing but the liturgy of that Church which had been essentially unchanged for more than four hundred years. What we had done was not to change one word in the Book of Common Prayer but, rather, to present the liturgy in a contemporary way. Nonetheless it seemed different and we had abandoned the high altar. There it stood, glowing and magnificent in marble and mosaic, surmounted by a golden reredos with the glorious figure of the risen Christ. To them, the altar and its symbolism had been abandoned for this new-fangled arrangement which jarred their sense of decency and order.

Subjectively for me and the others who participated in the service it had been a moving and wondrous experience. There in the midst of congregation and choir we celebrated the liturgy of the Lord's Supper. When I looked out I caught the eyes of the worshipers; it was intimate, real and involving as together we made our confession, recited the Creed and broke the bread visibly and offered the cup in full sight of the congregation. No longer facing a blank wall, priest and people were involved together. Gone were the hidden manual gestures and the hocus-pocus. Instead there was simplicity and dignity and a feeling of fellowship that had never been with us before.

Our first Sunday of liturgical renewal wasn't without its lighter moments. We had decided to follow what appeared to be the new trend by including in our service the ancient "kiss of peace." The kiss, originally a physical embrace, in today's most advanced liturgical circles is a form of handclasp. After a careful explanation in the Sunday bulletin and an oral description of it the reason for this innovation was given during the service.

When one of the young ministers went to give it to a deaf old woman in a front pew, she was heard to say quite audibly, "Why you nice young man, thank you." Then one of our most faithful and loyal members of many years' standing turned to the elderly woman next to him, took her hands in his and said, "The peace of the Lord be always with you." To which she replied, shaking her flowered hat vigorously, "Why Tom Allenby, have you lost your mind! Let go of my hands!"

Sadly enough, I could not comfort those who were emotionally disturbed by the change. I was the guilty one and the only thing I could have done to make them feel better would have been to make a speedy return to the old ways. I couldn't believe that their artistic peace of mind was more important than the reality of the new joy most of us had found in this simple change in arrangements. The faithful continued to come just the same, and some who had objected that first Sunday later found it had some attractive features for them. A few, a very few, took to visiting other churches, and one or two left never to return. One can only ask, what is important in the Christian religion, the action of the worship or the building?

11

| | | |

DEATH OF AN AGE

The life of a parish church is very much like a stream
which, viewed through a pair of field glasses, is seen
to wander in and out of forest and field. At the
source it is strong, crystal clear, as it begins its long
journey. As it goes along it gains from tributaries, large
and small, and the water gets muddy from time to time
as it picks up speed and erodes the banks which confine
it. The stream of a parish life, like a river, goes fast over
the shallow periods, passes over rocks and sometimes
goes over a steep fall at the foot of which the water
moves slowly around in a pool—a moment of reflection
—before it continues its journey. These are moments of
recollection when one can look back at where he came
from and look forward into the unknown course
that lies ahead.

Such a moment in the life of St. John's parish was created by the death of George Davidson, rector of the parish from 1913 to 1951. Under his long tenure of office the little redwood church in an orange grove grew into the neo-Renaissance basilica it is today. Every inch of the building has some reminder of his personal involvement in the edifice which for the man himself is both a personal memorial and a tomb. This magnificent church building is a memorial in that it is not only replete with artifacts he thought would add to the glory of the interior but also with personal mementos, which range from Dr. Davidson's portrait to his son's footprint as a child in a piece of tile in the patio and in the church itself. It is a tomb for him because, whether consciously or not, his personal investment of self and ministry in the building was out of proportion to what the real work of the ministry is in terms of people. Such is the tragic fate of more than one priest or bishop who has seen his own life and work justified in bricks and mortar rather than in the measure of love expended to bring new life and meaning into broken lives of mankind.

When I first went to this church it didn't take me long to realize that for many people who still remained faithful to the parish (whatever that may mean), the former rector was both a myth and a reality of some magnitude. At the same time I learned that his last years as rector had been unhappy ones for him and for some in the church who felt he had stayed on too long and who for one reason or another had found reasons to dislike the man and all he stood for. The fact that two men had served as rectors of the parish between Dr. Davidson's resignation and retirement and my arrival there was a help. Curiously enough, I had never met "Uncle George" as I called him to my-self, until one Sunday morning about six months after my arrival. I noticed two ushers escorting a man who could have been none other than the former rector to the front pew. When I met him after the service he was gracious and wished me well.

From that time on our relationship was a curious one, but one which held for both of us a certain significance. As time went on I invited him to have a place of honor at Christmas and Easter, when he appeared in gold cope and biretta to the joy of a faithful few and to the astonishment of the newcomers. When his wife died, I conducted the funeral, and the church was filled out of sentiment and friendship from the remnant that remained and many who had left the slum-encroached area that then surrounded the once elegant neighborhood.

While we never were what one could call close, we did have a bond which was based on a certain mutual respect and a degree of affection. From time to time when he was in the city I would call on him, give him Communion, or discuss some problem. He was always courteous, amusing and curious about the new kind of church that seemed to be evolving in his former parish. He certainly was not at all in favor of the liturgical innovations though he kept his feelings to himself. He had his own personal sorrow and bitterness which some-times came out, though in later years he somehow reconciled the great tragedy of his life and ceased to be bitter about the people he felt responsible for it.

Early in the summer of 1967 he had a stroke which put him in the hospital. I saw him a number of times

and found him usually smoking a cigar, somewhat
crippled but amusing and full of gossip. When the time
for my vacation came, I told him and said that one of
the other clergy of the parish would be seeing him
while I was away. He was grateful and we had a nice
visit. As I was leaving he told me a very funny and
quite vulgar story which kept me laughing even after
I had left his room. I never saw him again. He died the
next day while I was sitting in a jet enroute to New
York.

The arrangements for the funeral were made step
by step by the new curate, with the son and the few
members of the old guard who remained. Each day until the solemn High Requiem Mass I was consulted by
transcontinental telephone on the various steps and arrangements. The high point in ridiculousness was
reached over the question of whether Father-Builder
should lie in state in an open casket in the chancel. I
gave my approval. To my surprise this was canceled
because the son and one of the elderly attorneys feared
the security precautions were so inadequate that body
snatchers could come in and make off with the old
man's corpse. I must confess that this macabre fear reduced me to helpless laughter; and I have a hunch
that this unseemly merriment was echoed by Dr.
Davidson in the heavenly realms whither he had gone.

It was a grand affair, that funeral, and recalled the
age which died with it. As the vestments in the church
weren't considered good enough, the black-and-silver
High Mass vestments were borrowed from a friendly
Anglo-Catholic parish. A bishop was present to pontificate. And the old neo-Roman Requiem Mass was re-
enacted for the last time there—a sort of churchly
dance of death so dear to the hearts of old-time Roman

Catholics and their imitators in the Episcopal Church. While not there, I could see the whole thing in my mind's eye. The church was filled with those faithful to the man and all he represented. Not a few of the new members of the parish, both Negro and Caucasian, were there out of respect and, I would guess, out of curiosity at this re-enactment of a bygone day in the life of St. John's. They must have been in curious contrast to the rest of the congregation that day.

It was, unhappily, the occasion for a number of the old guard to let go of their feelings of anger at the new order of things at St. John's. The new free-standing altar, of which the majority were so proud, was the object of vicious attack and vituperation as this group of unhappy and bitter men and women vented their spleen. What they didn't realize was that, in all reality, their anger was self-directed at the disillusion in the death of a man whose life had, after all, been misdirected in terms of concrete, marble and stained glass rather than that intangible but enduring creation and re-creation of a human fabric that is the real church. In a very real sense this funeral was the funeral for an age and for a type of church which no longer had any place in the life of either a city or the Episcopal Church. That the anger should be directed at me, the man responsible for the new direction and in part for the new people who make the parish today, was natural and predictable.

While the three sacred ministers of the Mass went through their macabre ballet, the tears that fell that day must, for the most part, have been the bitter salt of self-pity as much for the loss of the man who epitomized a brief golden era of righteous self-esteem as for their friend and pastor whose aged corpse reposed in the expensive casket. In a sense, the tragedy of all the churches is present on such an occasion. The dead hand of the past lies heavy on all of us in our various religious institutions while all around us are sprouting new strong shoots of life—so often treated like weeds to be uprooted before they engulf the decaying structures that no longer relate to riot-torn Watts, rock-and-roll music and distances that are measured in terms of the speed of light.

Sitting by a quiet Adirondack lake the day of Dr. Davidson's funeral, I thought on these things. I could see the solemn recessional of choir, crucifers, torch-bearers, clergy, as the former rector's body left the church for the last time. I felt the loss experienced by those who loved him as a person in spite of his pretensions and foibles. I felt a certain personal sadness, remembering the times when we had talked intimately of people and the problems the parish experienced. Most of all, I was conscious of a lesson that Christians need to learn over and over again, which was shown in reverse by the life and death of George Davidson. It is the lesson of the supreme folly of the churchman, priest and layman, down through the Christian era, who seeks to build a lasting monument in the midst of a stream of history so turbulent that monuments disappear under its waters. The real things of religion that survive surmount the mad flood waters as a river craft does a stream that is sometimes perilous, sometimes quiet, with a helmsman guiding the boat through rough water and smooth.

The other side of the coin must be examined too. Who is to say that a thing of beauty created for a particular time in history doesn't in its own way contri-

bute to the fabric of the craft? For a moment in time
the frescoes in an Italian church, the magnificent carved
figures of Chartres' north portico and the joyous baroque of a Bavarian church—all have something to say
and to add to an institution that is historical and has
the dimension of eternity. Man, being made in the
image of God, is a creator. Therefore art, architecture
and music all proclaim the glory of the creator. So, for
the brief moment of their existence they shed the re-
flected light of God himself on a world which is in sad
need of beauty as well as love.

The sun sank behind the mountains of my lake and
the reflections of the pine trees on the water began to
lengthen and darken as I sat there nearly three thousand miles away as the final act in the drama of the
life of a parish church was taking place. The congregation would leave while the altar boys were extinguish-
ing the candles. The sexton would come into the empty
church and pick up the place, putting the bier candles
away for another day. The lights would be put out until only the sanctuary lamp remained—a little beam
in the semidarkness of the church building. One or
two people might come in to pray and light a candle
on their way home from work. Then when night fell
on the city of Los Angeles the doors of the church would
be locked for the night as the traffic surged by and the
city prepared for another evening, unaware and uncar-
ing that an old man had gone to his grave in Forest
Lawn, and St. John's had entered into a new period in
its life. The waters of the stream left the calm pool of
reflection and sorrow and moved once again into the
turbulence and movement of its inevitable course.

12

LOVE IN THE DESERT

In an earlier chapter I dealt with my rather subjective and sometimes negative reactions to ecumenical relations with some of the Protestant brethren. I also stated my deep conviction and commitment to the ultimate idea of Christian reunion. The roadblocks to reunion with the Protestant churches lie within me and my church as it is constituted as much as they do with the other churches that grew up out of the Reformation. Somehow we both need to get out of our skins for a bit and then perhaps real and solid steps can be taken in the grass-roots areas of American church life.

Now I would like to tell one of the most unexpected ecumenical relationships to develop between me and my parish with a wonderfully open and genuinely ecumenical Roman Catholic monastic community. It was not the result of high-level togetherness, but wholly accidental. Some people will say it was the hand of God. Who knows? Perhaps it was.

In any case, one Monday morning when my wife was visiting her mother I contemplated a rather empty day off. I could sit at home and read. I could go to a movie. But it was a lovely day and I thought it would be fun to drive out into the Mojave Desert with my paints to do a little sketching. Once out in the desert I headed for the foothills of the San Bernardino Mountains, where the juniper bushes and sage grow and there is shape and contour. I had trouble, however, because wherever I went to set up my paint box and canvas a terrible wind made it quite impossible to work, what with sand, dust and things blowing onto the palette and wet paint. So I gave that up and began driving rather aimlessly around. As I came to a crossroad I saw a sign announcing St. Andrew's Priory. I had heard of these Benedictine monks, because they put on a huge art festival each fall that has attracted a lot of attention. On the spur of the moment I turned my car into the driveway leading to the monastery. It was unlike any monastery I had ever seen. A number of farm buildings lay on the right; they had obviously been converted to uses other than that originally intended. Arriving in a rather large circle surrounded by buildings, old and new, I parked the car by a stone wall. Looking farther up the driveway I saw what had once been the original ranchhouse. On my left was the partially completed new building which, on closer inspection, turned out to house the dining room, kitchen and offices.

I stood there looking around and saw a small building likewise undergoing slow expansion into what would one day be an unpretentious, adequate chapel. Going in, I found a simple arrangement for the community services with a handcrafted fieldstone altar covered with some sort of unbleached cloth. There were none of the usual (and, to me, offensive) bad plaster statues of the Blessed Mother and St. Joseph. The only decorative touch in the building was a contemporary floor-to-ceiling stained-glass window behind the free-standing altar. I said a prayer and walked out again into the desert sunlight and the shade from huge old sycamore trees that lined the driveway area.

It wasn't long before a man in work pants, desert boots and nondescript shirt came up and introduced himself to me. He was one of the monks attired for his morning occupation and he offered to take me around. He showed me the converted stables where pottery and various artistic products were now produced. On learning that in spite of my lack of clerical collar I was an Episcopal priest, he insisted on taking me to the Prior, who turned out to be a delightful and gentle Belgian. I was invited to join them at their community Mass at noon and stay for lunch with such an air of charm and old-world courtesy that to refuse would have been discourteous. After an excellent meal I met quite a few of the community, though many were out on their various missions of ministry here and there. Sitting in the sun of early spring behind the dining room I talked with one of the Brothers and the Prior. Surprisingly enough, they asked me many questions about my parish, ending with a rather unusual one. Was there some way, I was asked, that they could be of assistance to me or my parish? Without thinking, I said yes. I told them I had been looking for a place to

take a group from my parish for a weekend. I found
myself opening up to these strangers my feeling that
we at St. John's had a real need to know one another
better and to have a chance for some open-ended dialogue. I told them I had an idea that from such a group,
and maybe even subsequent groups, some sort of real
renewal might begin.

I confessed to them that while all the new liturgical
renovations were fine and improved our sense of community at worship, real renewal didn't seem to come
just because we changed our ways of doing things in
church. Would they let me bring a group up to the
monastery in Valyermo and see what happened? Of
course, they said. When would I like to come? That
was the beginning of a love affair which has been going on now for over a year between me and my parish
and the Benedictine monks at Valyermo. Nearly one
hundred members of the parish have participated in
the free-wheeling weekends of unstructured group discussions, prayer and joyous friendship with each other
and with the monks.

Here we found a post-Vatican Council II atmosphere
of human warmth and literate understanding of
who and what we were as people as well as members
of the Church Henry VIII separated from Roman obe-
dience. It was on the level of our common concern for
the things that unite us rather than the things that
separate us which formed the deep and mutual feelings
of unity in spite of the areas of ecclesiastical and theological differences. Personally I felt accepted as a
bona-fide priest, and the people I brought were made
to feel completely at home as we and the monks attended one another's services of worship.

On Sunday mornings our celebration of the Holy

Eucharist was attended by various members of the community even though the official rules which separate us were strictly observed. We Episcopalians attended the community Mass and found that even in this area we have much in common as the Roman liturgy becomes known in the English language. It was in being present at one another's celebration of the Lord's Supper that the agony of our separation became most acute. To witness the same bread broken and offered and the same wine offered in essentially the same Eucharist was to experience in depth the pain and sorrow of the four centuries of separation. In our separate services we each of us prayed for reunion with an almost visceral depth and longing.

It was a joy to share with these men who follow the rule of St. Benedict their Saturday night Bible vigil. For us to study the proper Scripture readings for Sunday, to sing familiar hymns and to pray together in this context made a concrete reality the unity we do have in spite of historic divisions that still keep us apart.

It was on the foundation of mutual acceptance, sorrow at our separation, joy at even the limited areas of permissible unity and love that the relationship between the members of St. John's Episcopal parish and the Fathers and Brothers of St. Andrew's Priory has developed. Add to this, humor and plain human friendship.

Just as astonishing have been the results in terms of our parish life. Of the nearly one hundred members of St. John's who have participated in the Valyermo weekends there hasn't been a single one who hasn't been moved in terms of personal renewal as well as very real developments in our parish life. The formula for these weekends has been simplicity itself. We divide each group into four sections. Following a very loose schedule which notes the times of meals, services, coffee breaks and free time, the people have discussed whatever they have wanted. The complete freedom of discussion has allowed the people to tear apart all areas of church life which need criticism, change and new direction. Incidentally, the clergy are not allowed to participate in the group discussions. The sole role of the clergy is to give about three short talks which range from the state of Christianity in the modern world to the areas of challenge the Church faces today. At the end of each weekend the groups report their gripes, their hopes and concrete suggestions for improving the function of St. John's. These suggestions in turn are reported to the parish, and action groups are set up to put in motion many of the creative ideas coming out of each of the weekend meetings.

Some of the ideas may not strike one as particularly dynamic, but their results have been. One problem all groups feel needs correction is that of people not knowing one another even when they sit next to each other in church. This is not just a problem between racial groups but affects all the people who attend St. John's, because they come from so many different parts of the city. They see each other only on Sunday mornings in church and at the coffee hours. Now we have name tags so we can know one another by name. We have monthly parish luncheons in place of the usual parish suppers so dear to the hearts of American churchgoers. People don't like to come to the central city on a weekday evening, but they are all there on Sunday morning.

So why not have lunch together from time to time and really become acquainted?

A series of adult study groups came out of Valyermo. The church school has been completely revitalized. Lay participation in worship has increased. Inspired by the example of our Valyermo friends we decided that a festival of the arts would be a good idea not only for the parish but also for the community. Some of the existing programs, such as the clinic, got more volunteer workers, and programs for youth and the senior citizen are currently being developed.

But best of all have been the friendships which have developed as a result of people, many of whom didn't know one another, getting together on the parish weekends. To have met and had meals together, and to have discussed, argued and disagreed on matters as divergent as the rector's sermons and the problems of the ghetto seem to produce deep and abiding friendships which last far beyond a few days spent together in the desert. This, one suspects, is the real benefit to a group of Christians attending the same church every Sunday morning. Programs of parish and community involvement come and go, but the fact that members of even so small a group have come to know one another has made an astonishing difference in our life together. Horizons have been raised far beyond the particular problems of our sectarian life together. Low-cost public housing, the problems of urban renewal, public health, long hot summers, and ecumenical endeavor in and through our fledgling organization of the Greater University Parish—all have become vital concerns of parish life as a result of our weekends at St. Andrew's Priory.

13

| | | |

TO SAY GOODBYE
IS TO DIE A LITTLE

On the surface everything at St. John's was on the upgrade. New members were joining the flock. The ratio of Negroes and Caucasians appeared to be stabilized. This seemed remarkable to us at first until we realized that the physical beauty of the church, the music, and the presence of the University of Southern California were among the elements which kept us from becoming a Negro parish. Also, to my surprise, not a few of the new members came from the apartheid suburbs because they liked a church which was integrated.

So far as the community was concerned, we were involved with the Council of Churches, the Greater University Parish, and various welfare planning groups. The clinic was a concrete, though small, contribution to public health which gained us friends in the Bureau of Public Assistance and the County Health Department.

On Sundays there were more people in church though there was always room for more. The addition of two priests to our staff in the role of "worker priests" helped in many ways, and gave the congregation a welcome relief in the variety of preaching. It also gave us the illusion of affluence which impressed visitors! Parish programs went on even in the dead months of the summer.

Somehow I realized that we had long since passed the point of no return in terms of the few disgruntled members who might be categorized as the "old guard." With sorrow I saw them Sunday after Sunday looking glummer and more unhappy. The advent of the free-standing altar, the passing of the peace, seemed to them the straws that broke the camel's back. Nothing I could say, no amount of personal counseling, could make them like what for them was the final break with the whole tradition of the Episcopal Church and St. John's Church.

The fact that even more radical changes were in the offing only upset them more. There must be some parish somewhere which would keep to the old ways, they said, and they desperately fought to blind their eyes to the fact that change was coming and in fact was here throughout all Christian denominations. Ultimately there would be no hiding place from the liturgical, ecumenical and spiritual revolution of our times that is taking place in all the churches.

For me this became a great spiritual problem as well as a moral one. I was, after all, pastor to George Blunt, the elderly businessman who had in my early days in the parish given me wholehearted support. A devout man who rarely missed a Sunday, he supported the church financially as well as guided the Vestry in its money problems with a keen, though conservative, mind. Another was Harry Brown, a slightly younger man of great wealth who for many years had contributed much time and even more money to the financial life of the parish. I was personally fond of both of these men who had cheerfully made up the difference between a deficit and a balanced budget year after year before I came to the parish. At my suggestion, both had made definite pledges rather than coming to the rescue at the end of each fiscal year. Together, their contributions to the parish budget came to nearly one-third of the amount of dollars pledged.

If I hadn't liked these two men, it would have been easier to find some rationalization for their imminent defection. It was true that for the health of the parish as a whole it was demoralizing for the rest of the congregation to know that these two Santa Clauses would make up the deficit each year. Without them the members would have to go to work and discover what it really means to put their money where their mouth is. I talked with each man privately—not on the basis of his financial contribution but, rather, in terms of himself. George Blunt left first. From Easter on, he appeared in church only on what you might call state occasions, though he continued to attend Vestry meetings.

My personal fondness for George Blunt made this situation even harder for me. We had been friends. Many times we had lunched together to discuss the various problems and crises as they came along. If he had been a bellicose villain there would have been no problem. Essentially he was a gentle soul and his presence was always a blessing. In my last heart-to-heart talk with him I asked him point-blank what was more important—relevant Christianity or his concept of decency and order. George's moral and spiritual dilemma was naked when he replied that he knew that change was bound to come but he didn't like anything that changed the architecture of the building. Sadly, he said that he guessed he was wrong but he couldn't stomach the free-standing altar. He saw it as a barbaric innovation. With heavy heart I realized that his personal emotional investment in the building was so great that it excluded all other considerations.

I wasn't surprised when his letter of resignation as a vestryman arrived on my desk. It was a sad letter and in a sense pitiful. We had violated something which represented to him something far bigger, though he was not really able to put it into words. With heavy heart I read it to the other members of the board who received it with reserve and a fair degree of shock. We wrote the appropriate letter of appreciation.

Some of the others saw with me that it wouldn't be long before Harry Brown, the other old-timer who had so nobly supported the parish for many years, would go. He had always said if George Blunt supported any particular action he was for it. Now his moment of decision had arrived, even though he didn't say anything about it. And leave he did, with no letter of resignation.

At a meeting of the finance committee late in the fall, I wasn't surprised to find that the chairman had figured the finances for the coming year without including Harry Brown's contribution. He had done a good job of shoring up our financial defenses against this disaster so that we could continue without cutting down on either personnel or program.

The crisis had finally arrived. It was both a financial and moral crisis. The history of the parish was one of accommodation to the wishes of the largest donors. Here was the moment of decision. It couldn't be delayed. Of course, the easier decision would be that of returning to the old ways of worship. Remove the free-standing altar. Eliminate the handclasp which was the "peace" that irritated one of these two men. Had we decided in favor of return to the former ways of worship we could count on the continued financial contributions of both Mr. Brown and Mr. Blunt.

"Gentlemen," I asked the finance committee, "what do you want? Shall we return to the regular service or shall we keep on as we are now going?"

For a few moments there was silence as each of us looked into his heart and conscience. The discussion that followed would hearten any pastor who faced a similar Rubicon. When we were through going over the details of the forthcoming fiscal year we got down to the realities we faced as a result of this colossal reduction in income. One of the men who had been very quiet throughout then spoke. He said we must be grateful for the help and support Brown had given the parish over the years. But, he said, we must realize that his departure meant that the parish would have to do what it should have done all along—find the necessary dollars from the congregation as a whole rather than continue the economic bondage it had been under as a result of Brown's money. He said we must realize that we had catered to the whims of this man too long and that fear of his withdrawing financial support had dictated too many of the Vestry decisions over the years.

Nothing could be more healthy for the parish as a whole than to recognize that it must from this time on be responsible for its life and work. No longer could we sit back and accept the money and the conditions that went with it. It was a challenge he felt the people would accept and he ended by urging me to make the facts plain to the people in a letter. In the meantime, he urged me as pastor to be concerned and show concern for the man himself rather than his money.

It was the best sermon a layman ever gave to his minister and I was both encouraged and deeply moved. I know I felt the sting of tears in my eyes when he finished talking. I could only thank him and promise to try to be what I should have been all along, a pastor to Brown.

It turned out that the walls this man had built around himself were too great for my pastoral abilities, but I tried. Following the good advice I had received, I paid a pastoral call and didn't once mention money. I was received with grave courtesy as we talked of many things. But the net result was nil. As I left his house I had a strong feeling it was the end. Faith for him was connected with something to do with control, and his participation was more of an investment in eternity than with the work of Christ in the world. It was almost medieval and tragic in the sense that he missed the excitement and involvement in the process of a great design which could change the lives of mankind in the here and now.

As I left Brown's well-ordered house, I wondered if the essential problem and tragedy of Christianity

wasn't to be found in this situation. Culture in the form
of a man or men always seeks to mold the Church
into its own image. Jesus had been similarly tempted
when the devil offered him the kingdoms of the world
if He would bow down and worship him, and He refused. It seemed to me that afternoon that when the
Church bowed down and attempted to justify its position in terms of the power it achieved by such compliance, it ceased to be the Church.

I personally had been saved from the temptation by
the simple and direct faith of one of our laymen at that
finance meeting. Otherwise I might have followed
the course dictated by fiscal prudence and would have
lost my soul in the process. The human institution of
the Church today must face the loss of much of its support if it is to be the kind of church it was intended
to be. It can no longer continue to acquiesce to the cultural demands for conformity and noninvolvement
in the great areas of human need and conflict that cry
out for the hard decision of a love that is unselfish
and for a salutary sense of risk.

Returning to the church that afternoon I went into
the building and knelt down. A few solitary individuals came and went, saying their prayers and light-
ing candles. The late afternoon light gave a glow inside the whole church, even though the lights were low.
No tomb for the dead Christ, it seemed to me that the
light generated in this house of prayer was both divine
and human and couldn't be locked within the walls of
the building. It was meant to go out into the dark sreets
and the hearts of men; that new vision could help
them find new paths which lead to fulfillment, love
and adventure—or perhaps a cross.

And so a crisis of conscience for me and our people

had been met. Hard times might be ahead of us but I felt, that late afternoon, that we were free as a particular group of people for the first time. A load had been lifted from all our hearts. For the moment our consciences were clean as we faced the future. Once again my own personal faith was renewed and I knew that the role of the Church in the world is one of revolution and human renewal rather than one of acquiesence to the prevailing order of middle-class mores.

We had risked much but we had been given the strength to be adventurers and had recaptured something vital that our conventional Christianity had lost through years of compliance and conformity. I am not ashamed to say that there in the afterglow of the late day's light, I wept tears of joy that strength had been given me and our new leaders in the moment of our greatest need.

14

||||

A CELEBRATION

One of the shining ideas which came out of our weekend together at the Benedictine monastary in the desert was to put on a festival of the arts during the octave of All Saints. When the spokesman for the group which generated this idea talked about it he used the word "celebration." The plan was to devote a weekend for an art show, various recitals and a concert. As the weeks went by, these basic ideas got expanded to include a sidewalk cafe, a play to be given in the church, a performance by two teenage musical groups—one rock, the other Afro-Latin jazz.

As the time drew near, announcements went out to the neighborhood and thousands of people in the city and suburbs. A competition was held for young composers to produce a Mass to be sung as part of our service on the Sunday of the festival weekend. The celebration was to begin on Saturday morning at eleven o'clock. All day the day before and late into the night the people worked. The drab alley between the church building and the parish house was transformed into a street scene lined with gaily decorated food booths. Inside the parish hall the pictures of the artists, together with handcraft done by church members and our Benedictine friends, were hung and displayed.

In every sense of the word it was a celebration. The people of the parish who were involved in the actual work of the weekend had a good time working together. Many were tired, but I didn't hear a cross word; nor was the effort marred by the infighting which one finds in such church events as bazaars.

A few of us experienced last minute butterflies, wondering if anyone would come. We didn't worry long. Before the magic hour of eleven on Saturday morning, people began to arrive singly and in groups—people from the parish and people we had never seen before. By noontime the sidewalk cafe was filled with people buying hot dogs and other snack items provided by the food committee.

The sense of fun that was generated by the whole operation was contagious. Those who came as strangers were soon sharing the tables in the sidewalk cafe, drinking coffee and chatting with St. John's parishioners like old friends. The recitals were exciting and well attended. In the middle of the afternoon the loud and insistent beat of a rock band took over. Many of the older people as well as the younger element, went in to see what it was all about. The music was so infectious that it wasn't long before a number of the young people were dancing in the aisles and the oldsters were tapping their feet to the music they professed to abhor.

As evening came the lights in the church were turned on, and the floodlights in front of the church bathed it with a gala glow. The performance of Shaw's St. Joan, done by a small professional group, was so enthralling that the ushers completely forgot to pass the plate for donations. This was a minor disaster as we had hoped to pay the players out of the evening's take. Sunday, the second and last day of the festival, dawned bright and clear. The high point of the day, and perhaps of the weekend, was the celebration of the Holy Communion to the specially composed musical setting done by the young composer who had won the competition. The church was full. It was a happy service and the second time we had used the new trial liturgy. It was also an occasion in which we lived our liturgy with a love which went far beyond our own parochial life.

It is hard to put into words all that went into that service and what we got out of it. For me, the pastor, it was a sign and seal of the beginnings of a real renewal. I heard the full participation of the congregation when I greeted them with the age-old salutation, "Lift up your hearts," as they replied, "We lift them up to the Lord." At the time of the people's communion I saw them in the lines as they moved up to the altar to receive the Body and Blood of Christ. They were white, black and oriental. But more than that, they were people who in one degree or another loved their Lord and one another. The visitors that day spoke of the warmth of the congregation, particularly when their neighbor in the pew turned to them and said,

"The Peace of the Lord be always with you," and clasped their hands.

The other events of the festival went on right after the service. Those who hadn't seen the art exhibit flocked into the parish hall. Others went to get a snack at the sidewalk cafe. With almost no time lag at all the various performances took place. Late in the afternoon we began to run out of food, but miraculously the lacks were made good, and the weary workers kept dishing up hot dogs, cakes, coffee and punch.

Sunday evening we concluded our celebration with a concert in the church. First an organ recital by our organist; then some difficult and contemporary works by choir and organ. It was standing room only and a fitting end for our effort to relate our newly discovered joy in Christian fellowship to the city which lies outside the gray cement walls of our church.

In totting up the profit and loss I had to report to the Vestry that we had spent more money than we had taken in. For once in my experience no one complained. The consensus was that any effort which had given such pleasure to so many people was worth the couple of hundred dollars we had lost.

The Sunday after the celebration, one of our old women came up to me with shining eyes and told me what a good time she had had at the festival. As she left, she spoke these prophetic words, "St. John's will never be the same again." To which the only possible reply was, "Amen."

15

‖ ‖ ‖

NO SLAVE TO
BRICK AND MORTAR

It is said that the past determines the course of the present and that the present holds the key to the future. In a city church today it is difficult to see any shape to the future of a parish—certain trends present in the inner-city life and work of the church may possibly point to what lies ahead. My parish church of St. John's is certainly not unique in the present-day urban scene. Some carry on with small congregations and live on endowments set up by an earlier generation; others, no longer able to support themselves, are aided by their regional headquarters; and some quietly close their doors awaiting a commercial buyer. It is not uncommon to pass through the center of a city or a once stable urban neighborhood and see the bulldozers leveling to the ground a former house of worship for the faithful.

If one is to find any outlines of the future city parish church one must look at the inner life of any particular group of Christians as expressed in the new experimental programs they have developed that show signs of vitality. It is certain that the usual men's and women's groups of former years have become useless anachronisms. Likewise, the stereotype youth organizations, couples' clubs, and study groups only present a facade which has little behind it in terms of genuine interior vitality and outreach. We can fill our parish halls with Boy Scouts or other groups to give the impression of activity, but their effect on the life of the church is nil. Only the suburban churches can afford the luxury of a multitude of women's guilds and other time-consuming activities which give people the feeling that they are working for the church.

The first, and in some ways the most important, factor to consider in thinking about our urban churches, whether Catholic or Protestant, is that of size and expense of maintenance. Though we do not pay taxes on property used for church purposes today, there is an excessive cost of running these large and ill-used buildings. My own parish is a good example of this. The budget for St. John's, not counting our share of the national and diocesan assessment, runs to some seventy thousand dollars annually. This includes salaries, insurance, light, heat, telephone, repairs, maintenance and taxes on that part of the church property that is subject to taxation. Add to that about thirty thousand dollars, which is what we are supposed to pay to the regional and national Church.

To be honest one must admit that we could do the same job with a church and facilities of about one third

the size of our present building complex. How many
times have I wished that the builders of my church
building had built on a smaller scale instead of erect-
ing a near-cathedral-size building! It looks awfully
empty on a Sunday morning when the members find it
inconvenient to get to church. Granted we have a particularly beautiful sanctuary, but how much does
architectural and artistic beauty contribute to the *élan
vital* of the church. In terms of worship the only times
our church building is fully occupied is at Christmas,
Easter and a few other special occasions including our
concerts. On a "good" Sunday we have perhaps three
hundred plus people in the pews; there is an available
seating capacity of eight hundred. To be sure this con-
trasts favorably to one hundred and twenty-five of a
few years ago, but hardly constitutes an efficient use of
the space available. This is not only true of St. John's
but is also true of countless church buildings in cities
across the land.

The use of other church facilities, which would include auditoriums, Sunday school rooms, reception
areas, choir rooms, etc., fare little better in many
churches. They are used on Sundays and occasionally
during the week for guilds and outside groups, but for
the most part they are empty and useless. We think that
perhaps we have made a slight contribution by having
our space used by the clinic, Alcoholics Anonymous,
as well as various study, ecumenical and community
groups. As this is being written a theater group designed to give both black and white youngsters a chance
to learn something about acting is using the parish hall
seven days a week, to the horror of some of the members
and to the despair of the custodian. At least there are

signs of life, and that assuages the consciences of the clergy.

A former vestryman once said rather pointedly that all the counseling and office detail done by the clergy could easily be done in an office in the downtown area with far less expense to the parish budget. Of course, this is true; but then what does the church do with its rooms? This is a question which, to date, the city churches have not faced with any degree of realism or honesty. We continue to maintain our facilities, keep them clean and ready against the day when new uses may be found for square footage that lies fallow and idle much of the time. There are churches which have shown creative use of their available space in the development of community programs of relevance and value, and there are those who, lacking the imagination, simply give up and run a caretaker operation awaiting the final dissolution and death of their institution.

There seem to be two ways of facing up to this problem. One is to fill the church-house rooms with a number of unrelated or irrelevant groups that don't threaten the well-ordered life and quietude. Another is to open the doors to community groups and programs of one sort or another. Often this appears to be simply a desperate attempt to justify the existence of this church-owned space rather than a proposal related to any kind of well-developed church or community program. The clergy and parishioners who do this, however, are certainly not to be condemned. They have, at least, taken a step in the right direction. But the basic moral problem is left untouched and unresolved. This is the real question of the validity of the church occupying such valuable and costly space at the expense of the faithful, living and dead, who support the church out of their hard-earned dollars.

Perhaps this is an oversimplification. Of course, the church must have meeting and office space for its activities, both church related and community directed. But the question is, what kind of space should the city church have and what is the most productive use of its property in terms of the gospel? At present, city churches are slaves to their brick and mortar at a time when the Church needs to be flexible, adaptable and relevant to the very real needs, sorrows and aspirations of a rapidly changing urban population.

In thinking about the future of the urban church, there is not one but many suggested answers to the problem we are raising. The first is found in terms of the newly found unity among the various Christian churches. Ecumenical action certainly suggests that much time, money and real estate can be more efficiently used by combining resources. In many areas one big church building and large parish-house facility could be used by two or three churches for their day-to-day work, their joint efforts in community action and program. Even without the advent of the Kingdom of God we could easily share worship facilities on Sunday at different hours. Combine three or four churches the size of St. John's or even smaller and you have a budget of two hundred thousand dollars for programs which would be much more effective than our present individual efforts.

Another approach would be for individual denominations to begin by combining the work of several blighted churches in one site. With highly mobile pop-

ulations in our cities the existence of many neighborhood churches is a sinful waste of our time, talent and
money. The buildings and land of the surveyed
churches could be sold or leased to the profit of the
newly combined congregations. We can no longer
afford the luxury of many churches in urban areas.

It follows that a large number of churches should be
abolished entirely when they reach the point of no
longer having any visible usefulness. These churches
must cost their denominational bodies millions of dollars annually and are maintained, so far as one can see,
in order to keep up the statistical facade of the denominations and communions involved. To be sure there is
more in the life of the Church than a numbers game;
nonetheless there are countless church buildings being
maintained to save face. It is, of course, highly probable
that in the next decade or so all church properties will
become subject to real estate taxation. That would
force the decision, but one would hope that long before this becomes a fact, the major Christian bodies in
the United States would either dispose of these dead
properties or turn them to more profitable use.

What we are really talking about here is not economy
or good business procedures, but rather something pro-
foundly theological. At the very center of our Christian
religion lies a basic principal which applies to our personal and corporate life in the here and now as well as
in the future life. We must die in order to be reborn.
This is true of the institutional life of the Church as well
as individuals. If Jesus had not died on the Cross,
he could not have been resurrected from the dead. We,
the Church, must in this day and age shed much of the
furniture we have been caring for and carrying with us

too long. It is possible that the very wealth and possessions of the contemporary Church are not only an
affront to God but a stumbling block in the work of
salvation that we have been given to do. The Church,
too, must die in order to be reborn.

The churches must divest themselves of much of
their trappings and die to their pretensions of power
and prestige if they are going to move into the age that
lies at our doorstep. We cannot attempt to meet the
problems of this age of scientific advance and technological wonders, an age which moves at the speed of
sound if not the speed of light, weighed down by the
heavy weights of an age-long past. Ecclesiastical pomp
and circumstance is absurd side by side with a jet
plane or a man in a space suit.

Along with this must come a new humility. No
longer is the minister the all-knowing man who knows
all the answers to life and death. The minister must
learn the present age by rubbing shoulders with the
poor, the technician, the day laborer, the banker and
the computer analyst. It may well be that the so-
called worker-priest of the present day, the secularly
employed minister, will constitute the bulk of the
Christian ministry before the twenty-first century arrives.

As the great and unused edifices are leveled to
make room for new office buildings, parking lots or
bowling alleys, it is entirely possible that new and vital
congregations will be found meeting in the homes of
church members. Instead of people coming to the
church for the preaching of the Word and for the sacraments, if may well come to pass that the Church will go
to the homes where its people live. Certainly in

the slums and ghettos of our land, the Church would
be a more effective instrument of God's grace were it
to be found meeting in the kitchens and living rooms.
The mystery of Christ's presence in the Holy Communion does not depend on Mass being celebrated amid the
medieval or contemporary buildings of concrete and
stained glass. The needs of the ministry are simple indeed: water for Baptism, and bread and wine for the
Communion. If we can learn to travel light and fast
and not depend on our ecclesiastical crutches, perhaps
we Christians can once again find the real means to
change the hearts and minds of men.

All this will not be easy and I, for one, would senti-
mentally miss the beauty of our churches and the glory
of our liturgies. But we have too long put the cart before the horse in our religion. We have cared more for
our buildings, our ways of doing things and our institutional pride than for the saving work of Christ. If
you don't believe this, ask your clergyman how many
hours he spends in administrative chores, useless meetings and fruitless petting of cantankerous parishioners
as contrasted with the hours he spends counseling,
praying with people, and working to relieve the spiritual and physical miseries of his flock.

As the Church begins its radical revolution and renewal in its organizational and spiritual life, it cannot
well forget the injunction of its Founder, who sought
to bring salvation to those who stood without the ancient structures of Judaism. Our mission is to the whole
of mankind. Our ministry is to the stranger, the crimi-
nal, the lost and sick, whether he is a church member
or not—not as a lady bountiful but as a fellow human
being who can give the love that has been given him

by Christ without asking for repayment. The world is sick and tired of the Church asking for money for this cause and that regardless of its usefulness or worthiness; and the new age is disgusted by the Church's asking for money to maintain itself in the style to which it has become accustomed.

For too long the Church has ignored the poverty of its Founder as it gathered to itself the wealth and power of the world. Only when the church can rid itself of ecclesiastical grandeur can it rediscover the true role and mission of Christianity in a world which hungers for the word of truth and the sacrament of meaning.

16

THE ALTERNATIVE
TO DEATH

A great lady I know lies dying—slowly, gracefully and fully in command of herself. She is in her eighties, and her time on earth is coming to an end. Her life has been full. She has children, grandchildren and a few great-grandchildren. Though she professes only a vague church connection, her faith has run like a strong and steady undercurrent in her life ever since I first knew her so many years ago. Her death will occasion no headlines in the press and will be noted little by the world at large. Her greatness lies in her life, which has been distinguished by a gentle and self-giving love that has flowed freely to her children and all who have known her. And this love and gentleness has had the strength of steel. This is her legacy.

It would seem that in contemplating the death of a

person one sees two aspects of immortality. The first is the quality of the personal legacy which continues in friends and family and sometimes in those who have only heard of the person. Sometimes this is love; sometimes it is hatred; and sometimes something so creative that it starts a chain reaction which can go on for hundreds of years. Such persons as St. Francis of Assisi, Martin Luther, Karl Marx, Abraham Lincoln and Thomas Jefferson have left the world legacies which continue to move men and nations long after their personal histories came to an end. For the Christian the second aspect of immortality lies in the belief in a future life beyond physical death. Though much has been written on this subject and though Christians have tried to draw up road maps for eternity, the truth is that our only knowledge of life beyond death comes from our faith in God and our belief that all creation has some meaning . . . some purpose. Quite simply we Christians believe that life has meaning beyond the brief span of time between birth and death. It is quite futile and probably foolish to go much beyond this simple act of faith.

When confronted by the death of a person we love we are too often torn by our own sense of personal loss to think of the living legacies or the future of that individual soul in life beyond the limits of our earthbound sight. If we take our Christianity seriously, we cannot mourn for long. At the very center of our religion lies a basic principal that applies to our life in the here and now as well as in the future life: we must die in order to be reborn. This is true of our temporal existence as well as in the ultimate sense of our physical death and spiritual rebirth. We die (not once but many times) to what we were before our encounter with Jesus Christ, and we are reborn to a new life in him through the community we call the Church in whatever form we may find it. It follows that we believe that in dying physically we will be reborn in a new and fascinating life beyond time and space. We believe that this creative and re-creative process has something to do with God's love and our response to it. Love is the creative force through which God's purpose for us and his creation is operative.

So far as we know, it is not given to individual souls to be born again into earthly life. However, in the history of mankind, only one institution survives like the phoenix in a continuing process of death and rebirth. This is the Church. In its nearly two thousand year history, it has had many deaths and many rebirths . . . moments of greatness and moments of corruption. Alone of human organizations it has the capacity of regeneration. Such a time is the present. Everywhere one looks at the Church around the world one can see signs of the torment and agony of change from which new life will come. From the great Roman Catholic institution to the store-front church one can see and feel the strong movements of change as Christians driven by the Spirit of God seek to find new ways of living and communicating the gospel.

On Sunday morning at St. John's, I look at the congregation, black and white, and see the movements of the new trial liturgy in which we all participate, and I can sense the tremendous change taking place in this once staid Episcopal parish. This is particularly true as the members greet one another with the handclasp known as the "Peace." A new feeling of joy and love is moving in to take the place of decency and order, which for too many years made Episcopalians known as God's frozen people. The change in the worship service is not unrelated to the new outreach of the Church into the community. It seems to be a truth for Christian bodies that as they find new relatedness to life around them, and as they seek to find new purpose for their common work, the dimension of love enters into the very blood stream of the institution.

This is a time when it would be interesting to be able to look into a crystal ball to see what lies ahead. But there are certain signs and symptoms which certainly can give a vague outline of what the Church of the twenty-first century may look like. What will emerge ultimately as the reborn Church cannot be drawn in any detail, but we can predict from the current struggle without fear of contradiction that it will be radically changed in outward form and inward direction from the church around the corner where we first learned to recite the Lord's Prayer and the Ten Commandments. We can also predict that what is yet to be born will not come to life without pain and suffering.

We live in a time of radical change in our way of living—technology, communications, transportation and so on. Hardly a day passes that the newspapers don't carry some story of some new technique which will change some aspect of our life. The biggest change, however, in our American life is to be found in the polarization of our social and political life. More and more Americans are choosing sides which are roughly described as liberal and conservative. It is not surprising that this polarization is also taking place in our churches. There are Catholics who resist the changes begun in the Second Vatican Council; there are Protestants who deplore the avant-garde works of young ministers in the antiwar movement, the Negro revolution and other social causes. There are many American Christians who say that the old religion is good enough for them and any change of the old order is destroying Christian witness, morality and the very fabric of American life. If the present symptoms are indications at all of what lies ahead in the immediate future, one can predict with a fair degree of accuracy that we are going to see the more conservative elements separating themselves from their churches into splinter groups or sects. Some will in all probability divorce themselves from any Christian body and join the ranks of the pseudoreligions of our culture. Although it is probable that the numbers of the disaffected will be small in contrast to the total number in any Christian group, it will mean loss of income and will lead to an attack on the churches in the form of taxation of church properties and perhaps other forms of attrition.

All this will have its effect on the future shape of the Church both in terms of its physical form and its government, which certainly cannot be adequately predicted at the moment. Far more important in terms of the life and mission of Christianity are the more positive forces at work today, which more and more tend to shape the Christian Church into a world-wide organization. For centuries, Christianity has not only been fragmented by sectarianism but also divided into national and regional groupings.

Probably the first and most important factor that is moving Christians into a world-wide community of love and action is the matter of instant communications and jet-age travel. What happens in Tokyo, Moscow, Capetown, Paris or Selma is known within seconds around the world. Through rapid methods of travel in our world today, the physical isolation of peoples (including Christians) is ending, and we can know and meet one another as never before in history. Rapid communication and travel has had its part in the development of the new impetus for Christian unity. As we are able to meet and communicate, our differences of geography, theology and past history begin to become unimportant under the forces of contemporary history, which have begun to force Christians out of their self-sufficient and separate houses.

It is a Christian belief that the Holy Spirit of God moves in history and in the Church leading people to truth and meaning. For us who are blessed to live in this wonderful period of history, the work of the Spirit is evident in the whole ferment of men and nations as well as in the smaller worlds of the Christian communities. That the Spirit should be leading us toward a genuine unity of belief and purpose is seen in the new directions of Christian life and work as well as in the rarified areas of theological inquiry. It is easier than ever before for Christians to combine their efforts in the troubled areas of our American life such as race, poverty, and social and political action. In dozens of cities across the land it is commonplace to see Catholics and Protestants and Jews combining forces to combat the social evils of our day. They walk together in protest marches; they work together in the slums; and more and more they are seen to worship together as their common concerns draw them together.

Today we are seeing the Christian churches in an

agony of self-appraisal in the areas of moral theology. This is evident in the problems of family planning and birth control in the Roman Catholic Communion; pre-marital sex, divorce and common-law relationships are matters of serious concern for the Protestant theologians. The matter of human freedom of choice and conscience is today a major inquiry on the part of all Christians. These and the more obvious problems of our social structure are once again at the center of our concern rather than our self-glorification and self-concern for our church institutions.

What will come out of our concern one cannot guess. But we can hope that in the whole field of human morality, a new and clear concept based on the law of love will emerge rather than new methods of condemnation and penalty. For a religion that was founded on the idea that sinful man could receive forgiveness and a new life in Christ, Christianity has spent an awful amount of time, talent and energy defining grades of sin and human depravity. The churches have had the absurd self-conceit to think that they could be God in the matter of judgment and condemnation—even to the extent that they have stated categorically who will go to hell and who will go to heaven. God must have a glorious sense of humor to have put up with such human pretensions!

As the frontiers of geography and space are overcome by man, and as the new technology offers new and fulfilling life for all mankind, so the Church moves into a new age. Hopefully the Church will offer a new and abundant life of the spirit which can give meaning and purpose to man's scientific advance. As the Church sheds itself of its encumbrances of history and self-esteem, it will once again be the Church of the people of God and become the yeast in the bread of human life. All the signs of the present lead to the belief that the Church of the immediate future will emerge united in a common faith if not structure, dedicated to the law of love given us by Jesus. The portents of our present crisis of faith point to new and exciting ways of being people who are involved in the whole of life and participants in the process of creation.

Water, bread and wine are the chosen means whereby God works in and through humankind to ever make new and reclaim for his own the men and women of time and space. At the heart of our religion lies the principle as well as the means for renewal through the eternal action and reaction of birth and death. Water of Baptism for those who choose His way of life, which regenerates and renews a human soul and body; bread and wine for the continuing nourishment of the body and spirit and the knitting together of those who love Him and one another. Ours is a way of love which can free mankind from the bondage of war, famine, disease and slavery.

The Church which lies almost within our sight could be the revolutionary force which might forever change the course of human history. Given a true renewal and freed from the chains of self-interest and the last vestiges of arbitrary spiritual power, the Church could offer to mankind the only alternative to self-destruction and death.

EPILOGUE

Dusk once again comes to the city. Cars turn on their lights and the street lights come on. A coolness replaces the fetid daytime air. On Hoover Street the two-block area between the Santa Monica Freeway and Adams Boulevard has been changed beyond recognition. The street has been widened and the buildings which held the bars, and the other small businesses, have been long since leveled. They have been replaced with new one-story concrete commercial buildings, which now house the five-and-ten-cent store, the bars and the market. Only the little taco stand has remained, ramshackled and teeming with life in the nighttime hours.

And only the people remain the same. Black, white and Spanish-speaking. In the early evening and into the night they do their marketing, buy their liquor or do their wash in the new and gleaming launderette. Their lot has not been materially changed in spite of the modernity of their shopping area. They are still either largely unemployed or rootless, without hope of either material or spiritual fulfillment. They come and go in the neighborhood, but they always look the same. For them the metropolis has given them neither a present nor a future hope of change.

The words "Cant you here me calling?" no longer spell out the despair and anguish of their fate for the passing motorists to see. But how long must they wait while the city spreads out into new areas in the mountains, valleys and desert like a fungus growth of ranch houses and apartment houses following the establishment of new and better industrial plants? How long will they tolerate high rents, bad plumbing, rats and a standard of living that shames our middle-class self-esteem?

We have already had ample evidence that the poor of our land are near the breaking point. In the cities across our land, in spite of the do-gooders of church and community, there is anger in the slums and ghettos. It is anger at the arrogant disregard of a majority who continue to buy new houses and new cars and new refrigerators while their brothers and sisters exist in medieval squalor.

Unless the fire of love is lighted in the cities of our country, the fires of violence, hatred and vengeance will destroy their rotten cores.